DO YOUR OWN THING

Activity Books 3rd Grade | Vol 2 | Fractions & Decimals

AF207845

ActivityCrusades

Published by Speedy Publishing Canada Limited

ActivityCrusades
activity books

FRACTIONS

Determine if the fractions shown is the same as 0, 1/2 or 1

1) $\dfrac{4}{8}$

2) $\dfrac{0}{7}$

3) $\dfrac{0}{6}$

4) $\dfrac{8}{8}$

5) $\dfrac{9}{18}$

6) $\dfrac{7}{14}$

7) $\dfrac{5}{10}$

8) $\dfrac{5}{5}$

9) $\dfrac{2}{4}$

10) $\dfrac{6}{6}$

11) $\dfrac{0}{9}$

12) $\dfrac{9}{9}$

13) $\dfrac{0}{8}$

14) $\dfrac{0}{3}$

15) $\dfrac{4}{4}$

16) $\dfrac{0}{4}$

17) $\dfrac{3}{3}$

18) $\dfrac{0}{5}$

19) $\dfrac{8}{16}$

20) $\dfrac{2}{2}$

1. _____

2. _____

3. _____

4. _____

5. _____

6. _____

7. _____

8. _____

9. _____

10. _____

11. _____

12. _____

13. _____

14. _____

15. _____

16. _____

17. _____

18. _____

19. _____

20. _____

Determine if the fractions shown is the same as 0, 1/2 or 1

1) $\dfrac{2}{4}$ 2) $\dfrac{7}{7}$ 3) $\dfrac{3}{3}$ 4) $\dfrac{9}{9}$

1. _____

2. _____

3. _____

5) $\dfrac{2}{2}$ 6) $\dfrac{0}{9}$ 7) $\dfrac{5}{5}$ 8) $\dfrac{8}{16}$

4. _____

5. _____

6. _____

7. _____

9) $\dfrac{4}{8}$ 10) $\dfrac{0}{5}$ 11) $\dfrac{3}{6}$ 12) $\dfrac{6}{6}$

8. _____

9. _____

10. _____

13) $\dfrac{0}{2}$ 14) $\dfrac{0}{4}$ 15) $\dfrac{0}{6}$ 16) $\dfrac{7}{14}$

11. _____

12. _____

13. _____

14. _____

17) $\dfrac{5}{10}$ 18) $\dfrac{4}{4}$ 19) $\dfrac{0}{7}$ 20) $\dfrac{9}{18}$

15. _____

16. _____

17. _____

18. _____

19. _____

20. _____

Determine if the fractions shown is the same as 0, 1/2 or 1

1) $\dfrac{0}{4}$

2) $\dfrac{3}{3}$

3) $\dfrac{7}{14}$

4) $\dfrac{8}{8}$

5) $\dfrac{0}{6}$

6) $\dfrac{4}{4}$

7) $\dfrac{0}{8}$

8) $\dfrac{8}{16}$

9) $\dfrac{0}{2}$

10) $\dfrac{2}{4}$

11) $\dfrac{6}{6}$

12) $\dfrac{0}{7}$

13) $\dfrac{3}{6}$

14) $\dfrac{9}{9}$

15) $\dfrac{5}{10}$

16) $\dfrac{6}{12}$

17) $\dfrac{0}{5}$

18) $\dfrac{7}{7}$

19) $\dfrac{2}{2}$

20) $\dfrac{9}{18}$

1. _____

2. _____

3. _____

4. _____

5. _____

6. _____

7. _____

8. _____

9. _____

10. _____

11. _____

12. _____

13. _____

14. _____

15. _____

16. _____

17. _____

18. _____

19. _____

20. _____

Determine if the fractions shown is the same as 0, 1/2 or 1

1) $\dfrac{6}{12}$

2) $\dfrac{9}{9}$

3) $\dfrac{7}{7}$

4) $\dfrac{0}{8}$

5) $\dfrac{8}{16}$

6) $\dfrac{0}{6}$

7) $\dfrac{0}{7}$

8) $\dfrac{5}{5}$

9) $\dfrac{0}{4}$

10) $\dfrac{8}{8}$

11) $\dfrac{3}{3}$

12) $\dfrac{5}{10}$

13) $\dfrac{0}{9}$

14) $\dfrac{3}{6}$

15) $\dfrac{0}{2}$

16) $\dfrac{6}{6}$

17) $\dfrac{7}{14}$

18) $\dfrac{0}{3}$

19) $\dfrac{4}{8}$

20) $\dfrac{9}{18}$

1. _____
2. _____
3. _____
4. _____
5. _____
6. _____
7. _____
8. _____
9. _____
10. _____
11. _____
12. _____
13. _____
14. _____
15. _____
16. _____
17. _____
18. _____
19. _____
20. _____

Determine if the fractions shown is the same as 0, 1/2 or 1

1) $\dfrac{4}{8}$ 2) $\dfrac{5}{5}$ 3) $\dfrac{9}{9}$ 4) $\dfrac{7}{7}$

5) $\dfrac{0}{6}$ 6) $\dfrac{9}{18}$ 7) $\dfrac{0}{4}$ 8) $\dfrac{8}{16}$

9) $\dfrac{3}{3}$ 10) $\dfrac{5}{10}$ 11) $\dfrac{2}{2}$ 12) $\dfrac{7}{14}$

13) $\dfrac{6}{6}$ 14) $\dfrac{0}{9}$ 15) $\dfrac{6}{12}$ 16) $\dfrac{0}{8}$

17) $\dfrac{4}{4}$ 18) $\dfrac{0}{3}$ 19) $\dfrac{0}{5}$ 20) $\dfrac{3}{6}$

1. _____

2. _____

3. _____

4. _____

5. _____

6. _____

7. _____

8. _____

9. _____

10. _____

11. _____

12. _____

13. _____

14. _____

15. _____

16. _____

17. _____

18. _____

19. _____

20. _____

1) $\dfrac{3}{6}$

2) $\dfrac{0}{5}$

3) $\dfrac{0}{7}$

4) $\dfrac{8}{16}$

5) $\dfrac{9}{18}$

6) $\dfrac{4}{4}$

7) $\dfrac{8}{8}$

8) $\dfrac{6}{12}$

9) $\dfrac{5}{10}$

10) $\dfrac{7}{14}$

11) $\dfrac{5}{5}$

12) $\dfrac{3}{3}$

13) $\dfrac{0}{4}$

14) $\dfrac{2}{4}$

15) $\dfrac{0}{2}$

16) $\dfrac{0}{8}$

17) $\dfrac{9}{9}$

18) $\dfrac{6}{6}$

19) $\dfrac{0}{9}$

20) $\dfrac{7}{7}$

1. _____

2. _____

3. _____

4. _____

5. _____

6. _____

7. _____

8. _____

9. _____

10. _____

11. _____

12. _____

13. _____

14. _____

15. _____

16. _____

17. _____

18. _____

19. _____

20. _____

Determine if the fractions shown is the same as 0, 1/2 or 1

1) $\dfrac{2}{4}$

2) $\dfrac{0}{2}$

3) $\dfrac{0}{7}$

4) $\dfrac{4}{4}$

5) $\dfrac{5}{10}$

6) $\dfrac{0}{3}$

7) $\dfrac{7}{14}$

8) $\dfrac{5}{5}$

9) $\dfrac{9}{9}$

10) $\dfrac{0}{9}$

11) $\dfrac{0}{5}$

12) $\dfrac{2}{2}$

13) $\dfrac{6}{6}$

14) $\dfrac{3}{6}$

15) $\dfrac{8}{8}$

16) $\dfrac{9}{18}$

17) $\dfrac{0}{4}$

18) $\dfrac{3}{3}$

19) $\dfrac{8}{16}$

20) $\dfrac{6}{12}$

1. _____
2. _____
3. _____
4. _____
5. _____
6. _____
7. _____
8. _____
9. _____
10. _____
11. _____
12. _____
13. _____
14. _____
15. _____
16. _____
17. _____
18. _____
19. _____
20. _____

Determine if the fractions shown is the same as 0, 1/2 or 1

1) $\dfrac{0}{6}$

2) $\dfrac{0}{8}$

3) $\dfrac{3}{6}$

4) $\dfrac{8}{8}$

5) $\dfrac{4}{8}$

6) $\dfrac{9}{18}$

7) $\dfrac{4}{4}$

8) $\dfrac{8}{16}$

9) $\dfrac{2}{2}$

10) $\dfrac{6}{6}$

11) $\dfrac{5}{10}$

12) $\dfrac{0}{4}$

13) $\dfrac{5}{5}$

14) $\dfrac{0}{9}$

15) $\dfrac{0}{3}$

16) $\dfrac{2}{4}$

17) $\dfrac{7}{7}$

18) $\dfrac{0}{7}$

19) $\dfrac{6}{12}$

20) $\dfrac{0}{2}$

1. _____

2. _____

3. _____

4. _____

5. _____

6. _____

7. _____

8. _____

9. _____

10. _____

11. _____

12. _____

13. _____

14. _____

15. _____

16. _____

17. _____

18. _____

19. _____

20. _____

9

Determine if the fractions shown is the same as 0, 1/2 or 1

1) $\dfrac{0}{6}$ 2) $\dfrac{6}{12}$ 3) $\dfrac{0}{7}$ 4) $\dfrac{3}{6}$

5) $\dfrac{0}{2}$ 6) $\dfrac{6}{6}$ 7) $\dfrac{4}{4}$ 8) $\dfrac{9}{18}$

9) $\dfrac{7}{14}$ 10) $\dfrac{9}{9}$ 11) $\dfrac{8}{16}$ 12) $\dfrac{3}{3}$

13) $\dfrac{0}{5}$ 14) $\dfrac{5}{10}$ 15) $\dfrac{7}{7}$ 16) $\dfrac{0}{8}$

17) $\dfrac{0}{3}$ 18) $\dfrac{0}{4}$ 19) $\dfrac{5}{5}$ 20) $\dfrac{4}{8}$

1. _____

2. _____

3. _____

4. _____

5. _____

6. _____

7. _____

8. _____

9. _____

10. _____

11. _____

12. _____

13. _____

14. _____

15. _____

16. _____

17. _____

18. _____

19. _____

20. _____

Determine if the fractions shown is the same as 0, 1/2 or 1

1) $\dfrac{6}{12}$

2) $\dfrac{7}{7}$

3) $\dfrac{0}{7}$

4) $\dfrac{8}{8}$

5) $\dfrac{6}{6}$

6) $\dfrac{0}{8}$

7) $\dfrac{2}{4}$

8) $\dfrac{0}{2}$

9) $\dfrac{3}{6}$

10) $\dfrac{0}{4}$

11) $\dfrac{0}{5}$

12) $\dfrac{5}{10}$

13) $\dfrac{5}{5}$

14) $\dfrac{0}{3}$

15) $\dfrac{3}{3}$

16) $\dfrac{8}{16}$

17) $\dfrac{9}{9}$

18) $\dfrac{4}{4}$

19) $\dfrac{9}{18}$

20) $\dfrac{0}{6}$

1. _____

2. _____

3. _____

4. _____

5. _____

6. _____

7. _____

8. _____

9. _____

10. _____

11. _____

12. _____

13. _____

14. _____

15. _____

16. _____

17. _____

18. _____

19. _____

20. _____

Determine which choice(s) show the shape partitioned so each piece has equal area. If none, write 'none'

1) A. 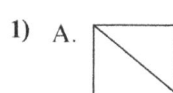 B. C.  D.

2) A. 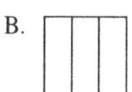 B. C.  D.

3) A. 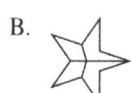 B. C.  D.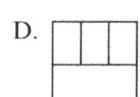

4) A.  B. C.  D.

5) A. 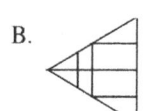 B. C. 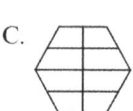 D.

6) A. 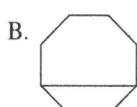 B. C.  D.

7) A. 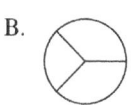 B. C.  D.

8) A. 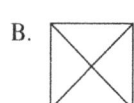 B. C. 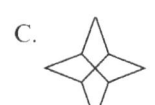 D.

1. _____

2. _____

3. _____

4. _____

5. _____

6. _____

7. _____

8. _____

Determine which choice(s) show the shape partitioned so
each piece has equal area. If none, write 'none'

1) A. 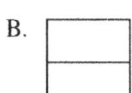 B.  C.  D. ⬤

2) A.  B. 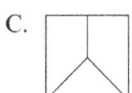 C.  D. ▷

3) A.  B. 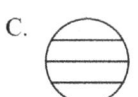 C. 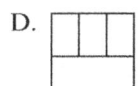 D. ▦

4) A.  B.  C.  D. ⬤

5) A. 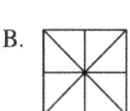 B. 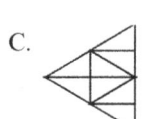 C. 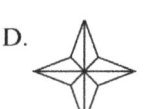 D. ✦

6) A.  B. ✦ C.  D.

7) A. 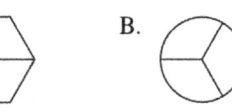 B. ⬤ C.  D. ✦

8) A. ✦ B. ⬤ C.  D.

1. _____

2. _____

3. _____

4. _____

5. _____

6. _____

7. _____

8. _____

Determine which choice(s) show the shape partitioned so each piece has equal area. If none, write 'none'

1) A.  B.  C.  D.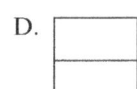

2) A.  B. C. D.

3) A. 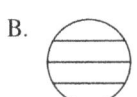 B.  C. D.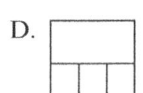

4) A.  B.  C. D.

5) A.  B. 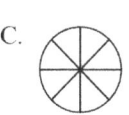 C. D.

6) A. 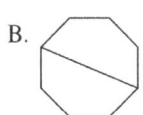 B. 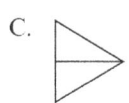 C. D.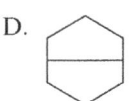

7) A. 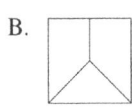 B.  C. D.

8) A. 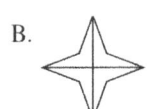 B.  C. 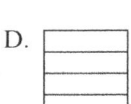 D.

1. _____

2. _____

3. _____

4. _____

5. _____

6. _____

7. _____

8. _____

Determine which choice(s) show the shape partitioned so
each piece has equal area. If none, write 'none'

1) A.    B. 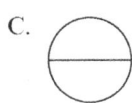   C. 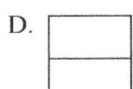   D.

2) A.   B.   C. 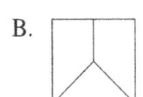   D.

3) A.   B.   C.   D.

4) A.   B.   C. 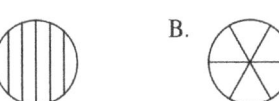   D.

5) A.    B.   C.    D.

6) A.    B.   C.   D.

7) A.    B.   C.   D.

8) A.    B.   C.   D.

1. _____

2. _____

3. _____

4. _____

5. _____

6. _____

7. _____

8. _____

Determine which choice(s) show the shape partitioned so each piece has equal area. If none, write 'none'

1) A. 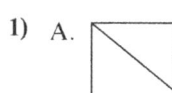   B.    C.    D.

2) A.    B.    C. 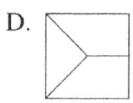   D.

3) A. 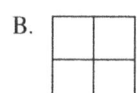   B.    C.    D.

4) A.    B.    C. 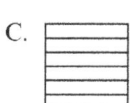   D.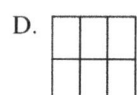

5) A.    B.    C.    D.

6) A. 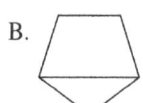   B.    C.    D.

7) A. 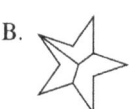   B.    C.    D.

8) A.    B.    C.    D.

1. _____
2. _____
3. _____
4. _____
5. _____
6. _____
7. _____
8. _____

**Determine which choice(s) show the shape partitioned so
each piece has equal area. If none, write 'none'**

1) A. 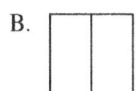   B.    C.    D.

2) A. 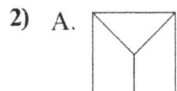   B. 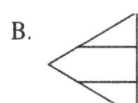   C. 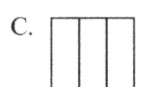   D.

3) A.    B. 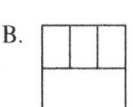   C.    D.

4) A.   B.    C. 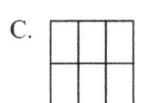   D.

5) A.    B.    C. 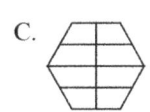   D.

6) A.    B. 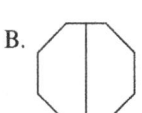   C. 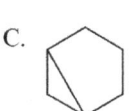   D.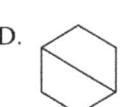

7) A.    B.    C.    D.

8) A.   B.    C.    D.

1. _____

2. _____

3. _____

4. _____

5. _____

6. _____

7. _____

8. _____

Determine which choice(s) show the shape partitioned so each piece has equal area. If none, write 'none'

1) A. 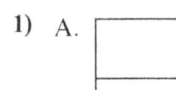   B.    C.    D.

2) A.    B.    C. 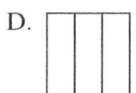   D.

3) A.    B. 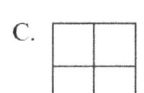   C.    D.

4) A.    B. 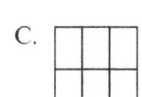   C.    D.

5) A.    B.    C. 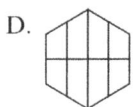   D.

6) A.    B.    C. 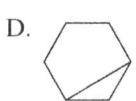   D.

7) A.    B. 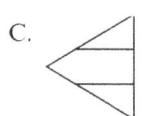   C.    D.

8) A. 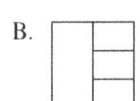   B. 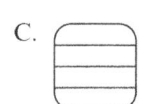   C.   D.

1. _____

2. _____

3. _____

4. _____

5. _____

6. _____

7. _____

8. _____

Determine which choice(s) show the shape partitioned so each piece has equal area. If none, write 'none'

1) A.    B. 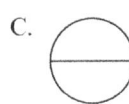   C. 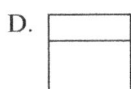   D.

2) A.   B.   C.   D.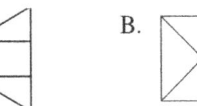

3) A. 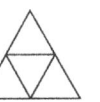   B.   C.   D.

4) A.    B.   C.   D.

5) A.   B.    C.    D.

6) A.   B.    C.   D.

7) A.    B.   C.   D.

8) A.    B.   C.   D.

1. _____

2. _____

3. _____

4. _____

5. _____

6. _____

7. _____

8. _____

19 Determine which choice(s) show the shape partitioned so each piece has equal area. If none, write 'none'

1) A. 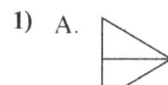 B.  C.  D.

2) A.  B. 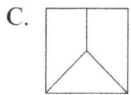 C.  D.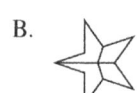

3) A.  B. 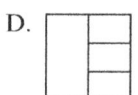 C.  D.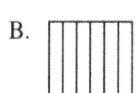

4) A.  B.  C. 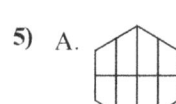 D.

5) A.  B. 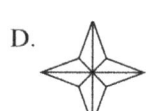 C. 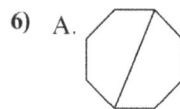 D.

6) A. 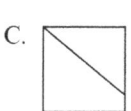 B.  C. 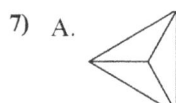 D.

7) A.  B.  C.  D.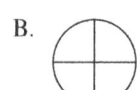

8) A.  B. C. D.

1. _____
2. _____
3. _____
4. _____
5. _____
6. _____
7. _____
8. _____

Determine which choice(s) show the shape partitioned so each piece has equal area. If none, write 'none'

1) A. 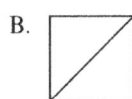 B. 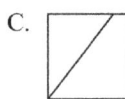 C. 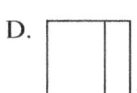 D.

2) A. 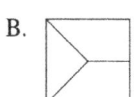 B. 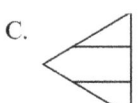 C.  D.

3) A.  B.  C.  D.

4) A.  B.  C.  D.

5) A. 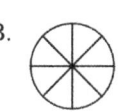 B.  C.  D.

6) A. 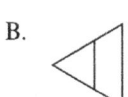 B.  C.  D.

7) A. 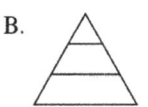 B.  C.  D.

8) A. 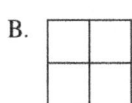 B.  C.  D.

1. _____

2. _____

3. _____

4. _____

5. _____

6. _____

7. _____

8. _____

Write the shaded amount as a fraction of the whole amount

1)

2)

3)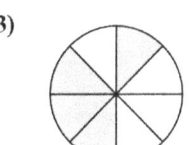

4)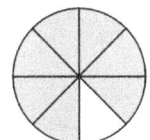

5)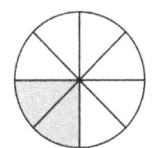

6)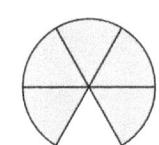

7)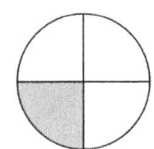

8)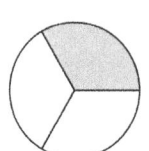

9)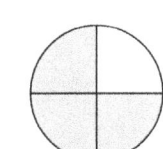

10)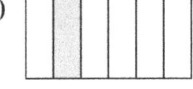

11)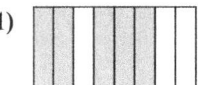

12)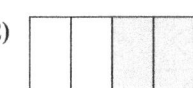

13)

14)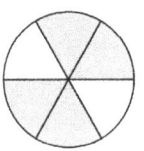

15)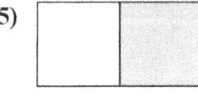

16)

17)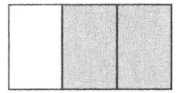

18)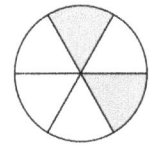

1. _____

2. _____

3. _____

4. _____

5. _____

6. _____

7. _____

8. _____

9. _____

10. _____

11. _____

12. _____

13. _____

14. _____

15. _____

16. _____

17. _____

18. _____

Write the shaded amount as a fraction of the whole amount

1)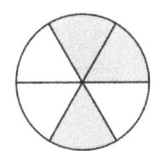

2)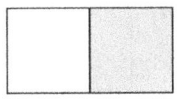

3)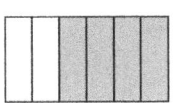

4)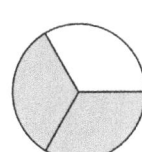

5)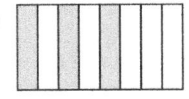

6)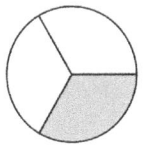

7)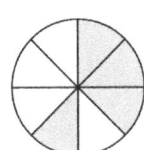

8)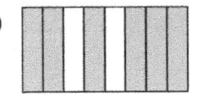

9)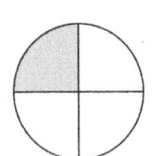

10)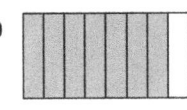

11)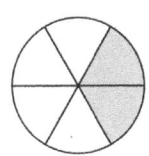

12)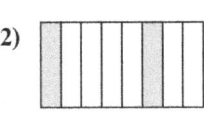

13)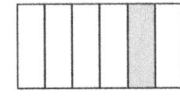

14)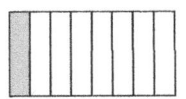

15)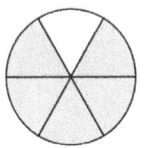

16)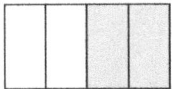

17)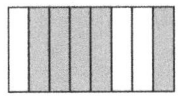

18)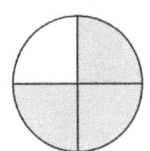

1. _____

2. _____

3. _____

4. _____

5. _____

6. _____

7. _____

8. _____

9. _____

10. _____

11. _____

12. _____

13. _____

14. _____

15. _____

16. _____

17. _____

18. _____

Write the shaded amount as a fraction of the whole amount

1)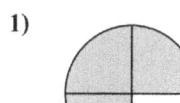

2)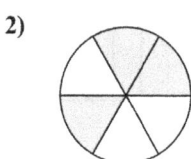

3)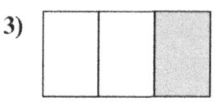

4)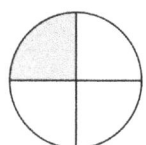

5)

6)

7)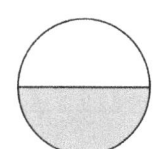

8)

9)

10)

11)

12)

13)

14)

15)

16)

17)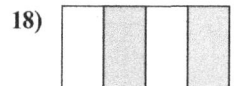

18)

1. _____

2. _____

3. _____

4. _____

5. _____

6. _____

7. _____

8. _____

9. _____

10. _____

11. _____

12. _____

13. _____

14. _____

15. _____

16. _____

17. _____

18. _____

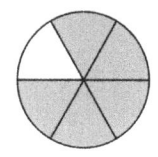

Write the shaded amount as a fraction of the whole amount

1)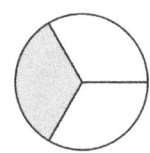

2)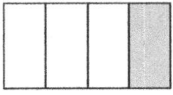

3)

4)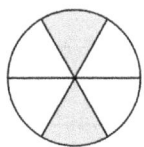

5)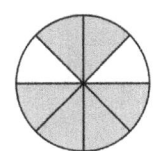

6)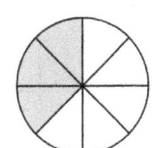

7)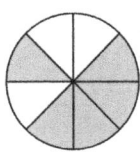

8)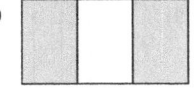

9)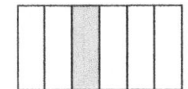

10)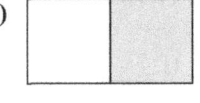

11)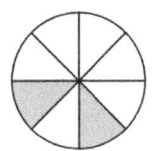

12)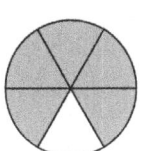

13)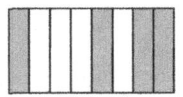

14)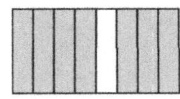

15)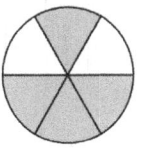

16)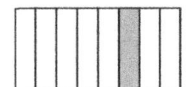

17)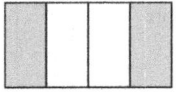

18)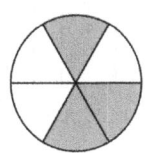

1. _____

2. _____

3. _____

4. _____

5. _____

6. _____

7. _____

8. _____

9. _____

10. _____

11. _____

12. _____

13. _____

14. _____

15. _____

16. _____

17. _____

18. _____

Write the shaded amount as a fraction of the whole amount

1)

2)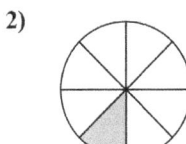

3)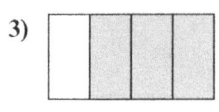

4)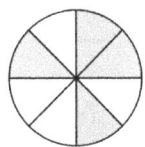

5)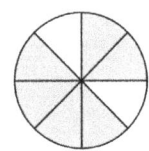

6)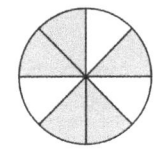

7)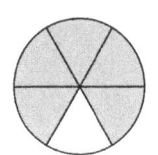

8)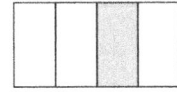

9)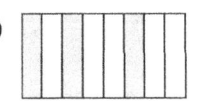

10)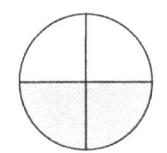

11)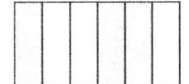

12)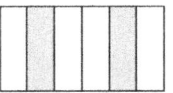

13)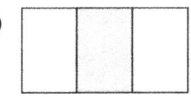

14)

15)

16)

17)

18)

1. _____

2. _____

3. _____

4. _____

5. _____

6. _____

7. _____

8. _____

9. _____

10. _____

11. _____

12. _____

13. _____

14. _____

15. _____

16. _____

17. _____

18. _____

Write the shaded amount as a fraction of the whole amount

26

1)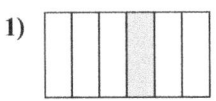

2)

3)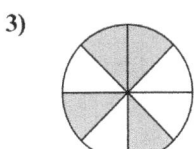

4)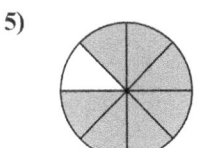

5)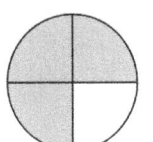

6)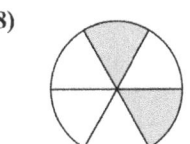

7)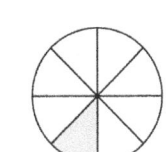

8)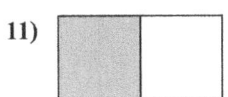

9)

10)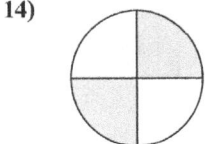

11)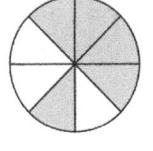

12)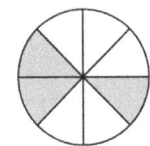

13)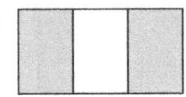

14)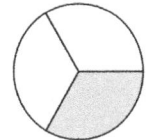

15)

16)

17)

18)

1. _____

2. _____

3. _____

4. _____

5. _____

6. _____

7. _____

8. _____

9. _____

10. _____

11. _____

12. _____

13. _____

14. _____

15. _____

16. _____

17. _____

18. _____

Write the shaded amount as a fraction of the whole amount

1)

2)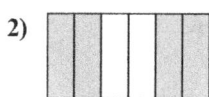

3)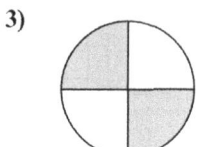

4)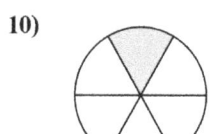

5)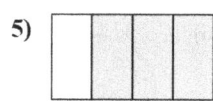

6)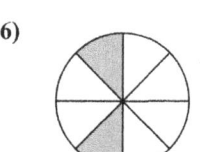

7)

8)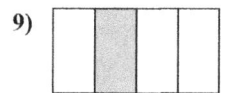

9)

10)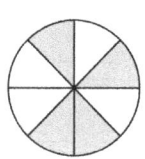

11)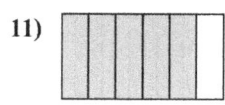

12)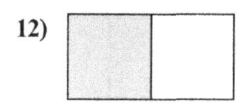

13)

14)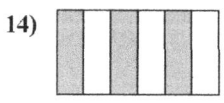

15)

16)

17)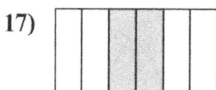

18)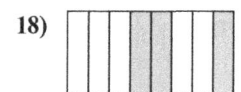

1. _____

2. _____

3. _____

4. _____

5. _____

6. _____

7. _____

8. _____

9. _____

10. _____

11. _____

12. _____

13. _____

14. _____

15. _____

16. _____

17. _____

18. _____

Write the shaded amount as a fraction of the whole amount

1)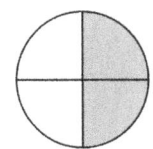

2)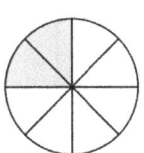

3)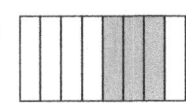

4)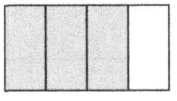

5)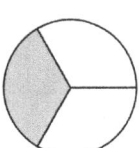

6)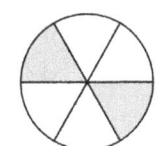

7)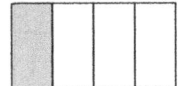

8)

9)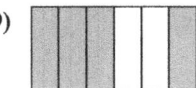

10)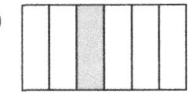

11)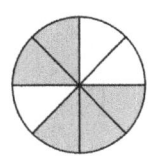

12)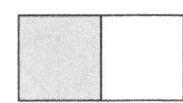

13)

14)

15)

16)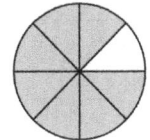

17)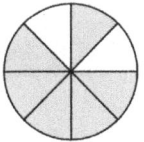

18)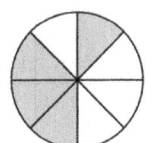

1. _____
2. _____
3. _____
4. _____
5. _____
6. _____
7. _____
8. _____
9. _____
10. _____
11. _____
12. _____
13. _____
14. _____
15. _____
16. _____
17. _____
18. _____

Write the shaded amount as a fraction of the whole amount

1)

2)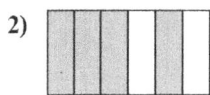

3)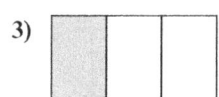

4)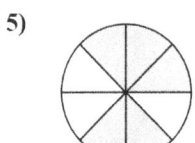

5)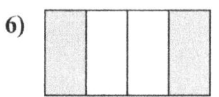

6)

7)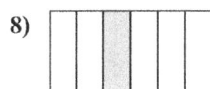

8)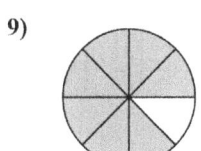

9)

10)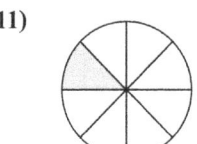

11)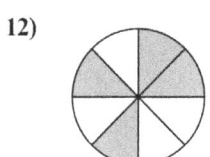

12)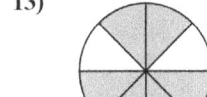

13)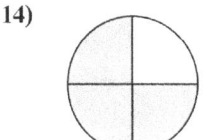

14)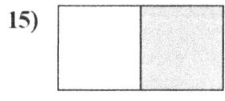

15)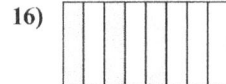

16)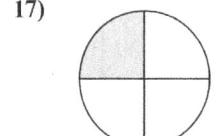

17)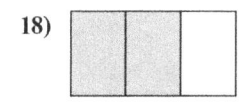

18)

1. _____

2. _____

3. _____

4. _____

5. _____

6. _____

7. _____

8. _____

9. _____

10. _____

11. _____

12. _____

13. _____

14. _____

15. _____

16. _____

17. _____

18. _____

Write the shaded amount as a fraction of the whole amount

30

1)

2)

3)

4)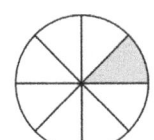

5)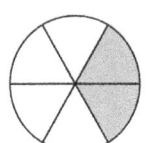

6)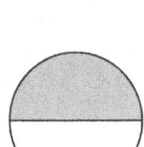

7)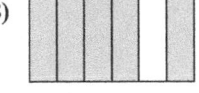

8)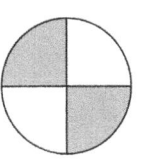

9)

10)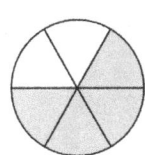

11)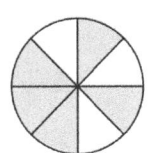

12)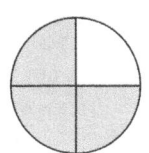

13)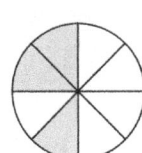

14)

15)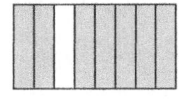

16)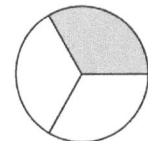

17)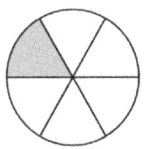

18)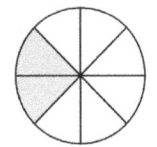

1. _____

2. _____

3. _____

4. _____

5. _____

6. _____

7. _____

8. _____

9. _____

10. _____

11. _____

12. _____

13. _____

14. _____

15. _____

16. _____

17. _____

18. _____

DECIMALS

1) 1.41 [ ] 1.41

2) -7.3 [ ] -7.34

3) 1.87 [ ] 0.187

4) -6.54 [ ] -6.56

5) 7.48 [ ] 7.42

6) -0.64 [ ] -0.064

7) -7.09 [ ] -7.13

8) -9.8 [ ] -9.85

9) -4.37 [ ] -4.39

10) 10 [ ] 1

11) 7.8 [ ] 7.79

12) 4.05 [ ] 0.405

13) -7.77 [ ] -0.777

14) 1.29 [ ] 1.25

15) -5.14 [ ] -5.14

16) 7.07 [ ] 0.707

17) 0.57 [ ] 0.53

18) 1.45 [ ] 0.145

19) -2.96 [ ] -0.296

20) -3.36 [ ] -3.37

Write the Correct Comparison Symbol (>, < or =)

1) -9.61 ☐ -0.961

2) -6.5 ☐ -0.65

3) -5.16 ☐ -5.18

4) -2.24 ☐ -2.24

5) 0.86 ☐ 0.086

6) 8.23 ☐ 0.823

7) 1.06 ☐ 1.14

8) 5.35 ☐ 5.42

9) 3.37 ☐ 0.337

10) -0.49 ☐ -0.51

11) 5.7 ☐ 5.68

12) -3.74 ☐ -3.75

13) -0.4 ☐ -0.04

14) 7.19 ☐ 7.23

15) 2.04 ☐ 2.08

16) -9.82 ☐ -0.982

17) 6.35 ☐ 6.29

18) -9.46 ☐ -0.946

19) 3.32 ☐ 3.35

20) -8.52 ☐ -8.59

Write the Correct Comparison Symbol (>, < or =)

1) 6.23 ☐ 6.26

2) -5.11 ☐ -0.511

3) 8.7 ☐ 0.87

4) 0.39 ☐ 0.039

5) -2.62 ☐ -0.262

6) -4.22 ☐ -4.15

7) 9.9 ☐ 9.9

8) 0.41 ☐ 0.41

9) 2 ☐ 0.2

10) -2.47 ☐ -2.51

11) 5.15 ☐ 5.12

12) 4.88 ☐ 0.488

13) 8.48 ☐ 8.56

14) -6.55 ☐ -6.57

15) -3.22 ☐ -3.22

16) -2.96 ☐ -0.296

17) -9.09 ☐ -9.12

18) -0.46 ☐ -0.38

19) -6.59 ☐ -6.67

20) 2.17 ☐ 0.217

Write the Correct Comparison Symbol (>, < or =)

1) -5.01 ☐ -4.99

2) -6.89 ☐ -0.689

3) 2.97 ☐ 2.95

4) 7.88 ☐ 0.788

5) 7.38 ☐ 7.35

6) -0.87 ☐ -0.087

7) 3.68 ☐ 0.368

8) 8.35 ☐ 8.35

9) 8.72 ☐ 0.872

10) 3.56 ☐ 3.58

11) 8.57 ☐ 8.55

12) -1.45 ☐ -0.145

13) -3.13 ☐ -0.313

14) -6.81 ☐ -6.82

15) 8.38 ☐ 8.37

16) -8.46 ☐ -8.54

17) -0.68 ☐ -0.67

18) 7.4 ☐ 0.74

19) -5.79 ☐ -5.71

20) -5.73 ☐ -5.71

1) -5.31 ☐ -5.3

2) 5.99 ☐ 5.94

3) -0.88 ☐ -0.088

4) 3.77 ☐ 0.377

5) 2.73 ☐ 2.75

6) 6.12 ☐ 6.15

7) 9.51 ☐ 9.48

8) 5.43 ☐ 5.4

9) -2.14 ☐ -0.214

10) 7.87 ☐ 0.787

11) -4.57 ☐ -0.457

12) 9.66 ☐ 9.66

13) -8.68 ☐ -8.66

14) -2.28 ☐ -0.228

15) 1.27 ☐ 0.127

16) -2.25 ☐ -2.31

17) -4.37 ☐ -4.4

18) 5.18 ☐ 5.14

19) -9.92 ☐ -9.9

20) -3.59 ☐ -0.359

Write the Correct Comparison Symbol (>, < or =)

1) 5.81 ☐ 5.8

2) 6.07 ☐ 6.02

3) -4.62 ☐ -4.54

4) 4.08 ☐ 4.14

5) 2.6 ☐ 0.26

6) -0.42 ☐ -0.38

7) -8.56 ☐ -0.856

8) -2.67 ☐ -2.63

9) 0.71 ☐ 0.071

10) -8.74 ☐ -8.69

11) -6.14 ☐ -0.614

12) 5.21 ☐ 5.13

13) 3.92 ☐ 0.392

14) -8.38 ☐ -0.838

15) 2.24 ☐ 2.28

16) 1.12 ☐ 0.112

17) -4.27 ☐ -0.427

18) -9.66 ☐ -9.7

19) -5.24 ☐ -5.25

20) 3.56 ☐ 3.58

1) -7.27 ☐ -7.21   11) -5.22 ☐ -5.24

2) 7.25 ☐ 7.3   12) 5.37 ☐ 5.39

3) -4.05 ☐ -4.07   13) -5.67 ☐ -0.567

4) -9.5 ☐ -9.49   14) 2.95 ☐ 2.94

5) 2.31 ☐ 2.37   15) -2.22 ☐ -0.222

6) 4.2 ☐ 0.42   16) 6.81 ☐ 0.681

7) 0.24 ☐ 0.024   17) -8.11 ☐ -0.811

8) 2.22 ☐ 2.29   18) -0.23 ☐ -0.023

9) 4.17 ☐ 0.417   19) -6.35 ☐ -6.41

10) -3.32 ☐ -3.29   20) 3.44 ☐ 3.51

Write the Correct Comparison Symbol (>, < or =)

1) -6.89 ☐ -6.9

2) -1.49 ☐ -0.149

3) 7.89 ☐ 7.85

4) 8.11 ☐ 0.811

5) -1.17 ☐ -1.16

6) 6.57 ☐ 6.56

7) -7.24 ☐ -7.2

8) 7.71 ☐ 0.771

9) -5.13 ☐ -5.19

10) -8.99 ☐ -8.96

11) 3.72 ☐ 0.372

12) -7.37 ☐ -7.4

13) 4.05 ☐ 4.09

14) -3.46 ☐ -0.346

15) 5.12 ☐ 0.512

16) 2.57 ☐ 2.51

17) 8.78 ☐ 8.71

18) -9.03 ☐ -0.903

19) 8.34 ☐ 0.834

20) -8.14 ☐ -8.17

1) 0.95 ☐ 1.01

2) 8.85 ☐ 8.77

3) -5.49 ☐ -0.549

4) -4.45 ☐ -0.445

5) 7.79 ☐ 7.84

6) -3.03 ☐ -2.95

7) -8.38 ☐ -0.838

8) 1.87 ☐ 0.187

9) 3.18 ☐ 0.318

10) 9.08 ☐ 9.13

11) -8.59 ☐ -0.859

12) 5.11 ☐ 5.1

13) -5.94 ☐ -5.91

14) 6 ☐ 0.6

15) 8.19 ☐ 8.24

16) -3.57 ☐ -3.56

17) -3.33 ☐ -3.26

18) 7.7 ☐ 0.77

19) -5.59 ☐ -5.54

20) -5.67 ☐ -5.68

Write the Correct Comparison Symbol (>, < or =)

1) 5.53 ☐ 5.54

2) -5.78 ☐ -5.83

3) 3.5 ☐ 0.35

4) 9.65 ☐ 9.65

5) -7.41 ☐ -7.39

6) -8.97 ☐ -8.89

7) -2.24 ☐ -2.2

8) 8.2 ☐ 0.82

9) -3.03 ☐ -0.303

10) 3.58 ☐ 0.358

11) -8.94 ☐ -8.96

12) 4.66 ☐ 4.65

13) -3.85 ☐ -3.83

14) -2.48 ☐ -2.52

15) 9.03 ☐ 9.07

16) -3.04 ☐ -3.1

17) -8.25 ☐ -0.825

18) 5.4 ☐ 0.54

19) 8.4 ☐ 0.84

20) 1.33 ☐ 0.133

Solve each problem

96.85	59.82	48.69	69.49	75.83
− 43.27	− 31.65	− 12.39	+28.69	− 37.85

51.82	89.89	97.98	99.29	30.41
+89.68	− 65.33	− 92.53	+82.34	+72.17

62.14	38.25	72.39	98.32	57.78
+98.16	+57.81	+82.36	− 37.92	+69.39

22.39	45.48	56.34	48.56	79.93
+54.69	− 17.85	− 51.58	− 40.77	+25.38

Solve each problem

63.55 - 23.41	88.98 +87.88	85.49 +46.31	94.17 +97.63	19.38 - 15.57
37.72 +57.63	83.37 - 56.74	68.84 - 52.56	90.82 - 84.34	47.37 +27.24
62.32 - 37.28	87.87 - 85.33	70.94 +44.75	57.22 - 41.42	10.95 +84.69
74.14 - 53.23	62.72 +42.67	86.42 +87.81	19.34 +57.83	43.15 - 14.77

89.29 - 38.61	89.99 - 70.45	83.97 +15.35	94.51 - 33.26	51.76 +75.97
85.88 +93.66	17.78 - 16.41	29.73 +35.12	40.16 - 26.24	52.78 +52.31
56.11 +63.91	81.85 +20.83	47.18 +27.66	42.75 +87.35	33.66 - 12.92
27.11 - 12.63	46.66 - 15.86	68.57 - 52.25	70.61 +28.14	34.48 - 29.79

Solve each problem

| 49.13 | 92.62 | 75.48 | 86.58 | 79.11 |
| - 17.43 | - 36.71 | - 13.94 | - 14.23 | +35.41 |

| 97.12 | 45.35 | 98.94 | 60.51 | 46.35 |
| - 80.56 | - 10.52 | - 16.97 | +45.54 | +81.55 |

| 28.99 | 90.62 | 12.82 | 34.54 | 92.99 |
| +50.33 | - 81.35 | +32.78 | +46.98 | - 40.97 |

| 62.71 | 88.92 | 65.43 | 84.33 | 71.64 |
| +81.93 | +50.61 | - 63.44 | +53.74 | +10.25 |

| 32.24 | 19.47 | 37.55 | 24.21 | 66.43 |
| +27.92 | +48.53 | +79.15 | +84.35 | - 48.78 |

| 42.83 | 11.12 | 91.98 | 82.12 | 54.16 |
| - 38.11 | +12.16 | - 41.27 | - 11.42 | +75.56 |

| 71.54 | 65.94 | 60.27 | 97.36 | 61.71 |
| +20.66 | +24.13 | +76.57 | - 35.79 | - 23.77 |

| 34.48 | 57.19 | 79.25 | 56.45 | 80.86 |
| - 10.83 | - 34.28 | - 42.14 | - 15.92 | +92.15 |

Solve each problem

61.46	84.19	18.68	99.87	14.91
- 24.32	- 64.18	+50.36	+68.25	+62.58

73.98	45.51	79.31	25.51	35.15
- 20.89	- 25.29	+36.97	+96.36	+72.83

73.61	74.77	82.38	86.19	60.24
- 36.48	- 11.38	+93.62	- 67.43	- 52.17

63.57	74.11	63.24	48.42	71.32
+96.15	- 70.59	- 44.68	+64.58	+57.77

Solve each problem

53.65	75.69	65.32	75.82	23.82
+71.28	- 72.24	+29.12	- 53.66	- 15.68

32.34	31.26	92.45	79.76	66.23
- 24.32	+52.31	- 76.72	+50.65	- 35.51

98.64	27.63	81.12	34.43	85.88
- 87.48	+98.63	- 23.19	- 24.73	+77.62

19.33	76.68	85.19	87.77	47.65
+75.93	+80.51	- 39.67	+27.92	+96.92

Solve each problem

39.31 +80.49	52.88 +45.36	68.59 - 31.67	25.57 - 23.38	61.28 +68.17
68.11 +26.19	80.81 +74.73	58.45 +88.63	90.46 - 74.64	49.29 - 14.57
39.59 - 14.19	52.31 - 20.96	65.36 +71.24	66.17 +99.15	79.43 +91.94
78.67 +26.83	43.46 - 21.68	44.67 - 43.86	98.77 - 62.22	88.25 - 22.12

Solve each problem

58.96 - 18.24	25.47 +46.16	82.41 - 69.42	65.81 - 47.88	20.84 +20.23
16.58 - 11.69	12.45 +90.75	58.42 - 49.49	41.41 +46.74	94.12 +92.92
52.83 +80.94	89.79 - 73.56	44.78 - 26.69	91.62 - 73.27	11.63 +46.26
65.73 +66.57	80.12 - 52.22	74.69 - 10.11	60.42 +36.38	57.51 +23.15

Solve each problem

85.83	32.57	85.91	63.51	60.88
+15.92	+72.96	+55.29	- 44.57	- 24.79

80.41	24.78	69.58	32.93	98.55
+79.58	- 16.31	- 54.92	- 24.64	- 28.48

81.25	30.32	22.89	97.62	82.96
+29.36	- 21.22	+72.97	- 72.44	+95.69

56.65	38.91	32.85	86.45	91.36
- 21.93	+76.55	+30.81	- 57.85	+18.14

Ex) A. 34
    B. 33.85
    C. 33.22
    D. 33.8

1) A. 73.96
    B. 73.5
    C. 73.4
    D. 73.1

2) A. 3.29
    B. 3.55
    C. 3.6
    D. 3.86

3) A. 4.19
    B. 4.27
    C. 4.6
    D. 5

4) A. 5.7
    B. 5.2
    C. 5.6
    D. 5.25

5) A. 22.4
    B. 22.8
    C. 22.3
    D. 22.91

6) A. 11.59
    B. 11.46
    C. 12
    D. 11.6

7) A. 8
    B. 7.96
    C. 7.35
    D. 7.63

8) A. 3
    B. 2.57
    C. 2.9
    D. 2.2

9) A. 9.17
    B. 9.5
    C. 9.9
    D. 10

10) A. 75.6
    B. 75.9
    C. 75.8
    D. 75.22

11) A. 83.11
    B. 83.6
    C. 83.16
    D. 83.4

12) A. 3.8
    B. 4
    C. 3.86
    D. 3.9

13) A. 72.5
    B. 72.59
    C. 72.4
    D. 72.3

14) A. 44.9
    B. 44.5
    C. 44.53
    D. 44

15) A. 4.2
    B. 5
    C. 4.99
    D. 4.22

16) A. 7.3
    B. 7.01
    C. 8
    D. 7.8

17) A. 3.68
    B. 3.5
    C. 3.7
    D. 3.88

18) A. 14.62
    B. 14.5
    C. 14.87
    D. 14.76

19) A. 65.8
    B. 66
    C. 65.2
    D. 65.7

20) A. 2.25
    B. 2.52
    C. 2.2
    D. 2.1

Ex. _C,D,B,A_

1. _____
2. _____
3. _____
4. _____
5. _____
6. _____
7. _____
8. _____
9. _____
10. _____
11. _____
12. _____
13. _____
14. _____
15. _____
16. _____
17. _____
18. _____
19. _____
20. _____

Order the numbers from least to greatest

Ex) A. 93.56
B. 94
C. 93.73
D. 93.2

1) A. 64.2
B. 64.8
C. 64.15
D. 64.84

2) A. 53.4
B. 53.22
C. 53.67
D. 53.42

3) A. 4.7
B. 5
C. 4.9
D. 4.56

4) A. 9.2
B. 9.18
C. 9
D. 9.7

5) A. 6.6
B. 6.29
C. 6.4
D. 6.17

6) A. 5.1
B. 5.4
C. 5.9
D. 5.5

7) A. 10.41
B. 10.4
C. 10.46
D. 10

8) A. 8.9
B. 8.48
C. 8.4
D. 8.7

9) A. 84.67
B. 84.42
C. 84.4
D. 84

10) A. 87.8
B. 88
C. 87.62
D. 87.6

11) A. 90
B. 89.9
C. 89.49
D. 89.5

12) A. 3.42
B. 3
C. 3.8
D. 3.94

13) A. 3.94
B. 3.48
C. 3.8
D. 3.84

14) A. 1
B. 1.27
C. 1.3
D. 1.2

15) A. 8.75
B. 8.48
C. 8.6
D. 8.9

16) A. 49.9
B. 49.22
C. 49.2
D. 49.61

17) A. 96.34
B. 96
C. 96.4
D. 96.9

18) A. 73
B. 72.59
C. 72.99
D. 72.86

19) A. 9.78
B. 9.43
C. 10
D. 9.7

20) A. 3
B. 2.2
C. 2.5
D. 2.42

Ex. D,A,C,B

1. _____

2. _____

3. _____

4. _____

5. _____

6. _____

7. _____

8. _____

9. _____

10. _____

11. _____

12. _____

13. _____

14. _____

15. _____

16. _____

17. _____

18. _____

19. _____

20. _____

Ex) A. 4.77
     B. 4.62
     C. 5
     D. 4.1

1) A. 76.57
     B. 77
     C. 76.6
     D. 76.66

2) A. 9.59
     B. 9.2
     C. 9.58
     D. 9.92

Ex. _D,B,A,C_

1. _____

2. _____

3) A. 39.9
     B. 39.17
     C. 39.26
     D. 39.56

4) A. 28.4
     B. 28.1
     C. 29
     D. 28.24

5) A. 5.58
     B. 5.5
     C. 5.62
     D. 5.7

3. _____

4. _____

5. _____

6) A. 54.4
     B. 54.52
     C. 54.45
     D. 54.7

7) A. 54.68
     B. 54.3
     C. 54.04
     D. 54.5

8) A. 8.84
     B. 8.59
     C. 8.1
     D. 8.4

6. _____

7. _____

8. _____

9) A. 7.18
     B. 7.7
     C. 7.79
     D. 7.1

10) A. 59.75
      B. 59.3
      C. 59.6
      D. 59.49

11) A. 96.78
      B. 96.55
      C. 96.8
      D. 96.6

9. _____

10. _____

11. _____

12) A. 6.12
      B. 6.2
      C. 6.8
      D. 6.17

13) A. 5.2
      B. 5.15
      C. 5.45
      D. 5.52

14) A. 75
      B. 74.45
      C. 74.44
      D. 74.59

12. _____

13. _____

14. _____

15) A. 85.5
      B. 85.4
      C. 85.01
      D. 85.79

16) A. 6.48
      B. 6.67
      C. 6.7
      D. 6.27

17) A. 6.32
      B. 6.3
      C. 6.18
      D. 6

15. _____

16. _____

17. _____

18) A. 9.3
      B. 9.66
      C. 9.58
      D. 10

19) A. 2.31
      B. 2.4
      C. 2.32
      D. 2.1

20) A. 3.7
      B. 3.72
      C. 3.6
      D. 3.2

18. _____

19. _____

20. _____

Order the numbers from least to greatest

Ex) A. 51.9
B. 52
C. 51.13
D. 51.7

1) A. 6.73
B. 7
C. 6.45
D. 6.5

2) A. 59.6
B. 59.03
C. 59.7
D. 59.17

Ex. _C,D,A,B_

1. _____

2. _____

3) A. 21.4
B. 21.49
C. 21
D. 21.89

4) A. 91.72
B. 91.9
C. 92
D. 91.58

5) A. 7.8
B. 7
C. 7.88
D. 7.44

3. _____

4. _____

5. _____

6) A. 23.18
B. 23.53
C. 23.48
D. 23.9

7) A. 42.64
B. 42.6
C. 42.3
D. 42.42

8) A. 5.74
B. 6
C. 5.88
D. 5.82

6. _____

7. _____

8. _____

9) A. 30
B. 30.13
C. 30.4
D. 30.3

10) A. 48.3
B. 48.94
C. 48.4
D. 48

11) A. 2.7
B. 2.8
C. 2.3
D. 2.82

9. _____

10. _____

11. _____

12) A. 47.5
B. 47.7
C. 48
D. 47.53

13) A. 37.05
B. 37.9
C. 37.72
D. 37.4

14) A. 2.5
B. 2.2
C. 2.93
D. 2.83

12. _____

13. _____

14. _____

15) A. 64
B. 63.36
C. 63.3
D. 63.4

16) A. 11.05
B. 11.56
C. 12
D. 11.54

17) A. 90.98
B. 91
C. 90.54
D. 90.1

15. _____

16. _____

17. _____

18) A. 7.7
B. 8
C. 7.41
D. 7.92

19) A. 9.48
B. 9.56
C. 9.4
D. 9.2

20) A. 63.95
B. 63.3
C. 63.7
D. 63.1

18. _____

19. _____

20. _____

Order the numbers from least to greatest

55

Ex) A. 68.1
      B. 68.47
      C. 68.4
      D. 68.43

1) A. 7
    B. 7.4
    C. 7.35
    D. 7.5

2) A. 89.95
    B. 89.8
    C. 89.4
    D. 89.37

3) A. 1.87
    B. 1.9
    C. 1.3
    D. 2

4) A. 96.8
    B. 96.81
    C. 96.5
    D. 97

5) A. 4.17
    B. 4.93
    C. 4.8
    D. 4.7

6) A. 2.18
    B. 2.02
    C. 2.7
    D. 2.38

7) A. 66.26
    B. 66.5
    C. 66.61
    D. 67

8) A. 37.3
    B. 37.58
    C. 38
    D. 37.22

9) A. 62
    B. 61.9
    C. 61.85
    D. 61.6

10) A. 38.89
     B. 38
     C. 38.8
     D. 38.08

11) A. 46
     B. 46.59
     C. 46.93
     D. 46.89

12) A. 90.1
     B. 90.2
     C. 90.4
     D. 90.63

13) A. 2
     B. 2.83
     C. 2.2
     D. 2.3

14) A. 24.9
     B. 24
     C. 24.33
     D. 24.5

15) A. 97.21
     B. 97.42
     C. 97.4
     D. 97

16) A. 26
     B. 25.74
     C. 25.9
     D. 25.1

17) A. 74.3
     B. 74.7
     C. 74.9
     D. 74.73

18) A. 3.9
     B. 3
     C. 3.3
     D. 3.1

19) A. 8.9
     B. 8
     C. 8.54
     D. 8.51

20) A. 4.12
     B. 4.3
     C. 4.93
     D. 4.1

Ex.   A,C,D,B

1. _____

2. _____

3. _____

4. _____

5. _____

6. _____

7. _____

8. _____

9. _____

10. _____

11. _____

12. _____

13. _____

14. _____

15. _____

16. _____

17. _____

18. _____

19. _____

20. _____

Order the numbers from least to greatest

Ex) A. 39.53
     B. 39.3
     C. 39.22
     D. 39.9

1) A. 3.9
    B. 3.95
    C. 3.7
    D. 3.74

2) A. 20.19
    B. 20
    C. 20.4
    D. 20.6

3) A. 3.4
    B. 3
    C. 3.24
    D. 3.9

4) A. 36.8
    B. 36.1
    C. 36.23
    D. 37

5) A. 1.3
    B. 1.37
    C. 1.5
    D. 1.2

6) A. 27.42
    B. 27.88
    C. 27.7
    D. 27

7) A. 2.55
    B. 2.6
    C. 2.3
    D. 2.67

8) A. 55.6
    B. 55.56
    C. 55.8
    D. 55.2

9) A. 6.59
    B. 7
    C. 6.6
    D. 6.5

10) A. 26.1
     B. 26.86
     C. 26.51
     D. 26.3

11) A. 46.6
     B. 46.19
     C. 46.8
     D. 47

12) A. 7.4
     B. 7.3
     C. 7.5
     D. 7.19

13) A. 8.23
     B. 8.7
     C. 8
     D. 8.4

14) A. 9
     B. 8.99
     C. 8.61
     D. 8.64

15) A. 7.9
     B. 7.2
     C. 7.04
     D. 7.73

16) A. 28.8
     B. 28.6
     C. 28.5
     D. 28.9

17) A. 30.2
     B. 30.37
     C. 30.82
     D. 30.71

18) A. 60.3
     B. 61
     C. 60.5
     D. 60.71

19) A. 61.9
     B. 61.59
     C. 61.84
     D. 61.91

20) A. 7.6
     B. 7.47
     C. 7
     D. 7.8

Ex. _C,B,A,D_

1. _____

2. _____

3. _____

4. _____

5. _____

6. _____

7. _____

8. _____

9. _____

10. _____

11. _____

12. _____

13. _____

14. _____

15. _____

16. _____

17. _____

18. _____

19. _____

20. _____

Order the numbers from least to greatest

Ex)
A. 5.17
B. 5.95
C. 6
D. 5.9

1)
A. 23.3
B. 23.4
C. 23.9
D. 23.26

2)
A. 7.5
B. 7.65
C. 7.97
D. 7.14

3)
A. 18.41
B. 18.83
C. 19
D. 18.5

4)
A. 14.36
B. 14.4
C. 14.86
D. 14.7

5)
A. 62.24
B. 62.49
C. 62.4
D. 62.7

6)
A. 1.72
B. 1.74
C. 1.52
D. 1.36

7)
A. 2.5
B. 2.4
C. 2.12
D. 2.7

8)
A. 73.75
B. 73.2
C. 74
D. 73.17

9)
A. 3.42
B. 3.7
C. 3.2
D. 4

10)
A. 19.18
B. 19.2
C. 19.42
D. 19

11)
A. 29
B. 28.26
C. 28.5
D. 28.7

12)
A. 97.6
B. 97.52
C. 97.95
D. 97.7

13)
A. 9
B. 8.3
C. 8.7
D. 8.99

14)
A. 50
B. 49.4
C. 49.83
D. 49.5

15)
A. 29.92
B. 30
C. 29.7
D. 29.5

16)
A. 9.5
B. 9.6
C. 9.57
D. 9.1

17)
A. 3.6
B. 3.3
C. 3.39
D. 3.8

18)
A. 4.4
B. 4.12
C. 4.41
D. 4.5

19)
A. 24.92
B. 24.4
C. 24.28
D. 24.3

20)
A. 7.21
B. 7.5
C. 7.4
D. 7

Ex. ___A,D,B,C___

1. _____

2. _____

3. _____

4. _____

5. _____

6. _____

7. _____

8. _____

9. _____

10. _____

11. _____

12. _____

13. _____

14. _____

15. _____

16. _____

17. _____

18. _____

19. _____

20. _____

Order the numbers from least to greatest

Ex) A. 68
B. 67.3
C. 67.6
D. 67.89

1) A. 2.1
B. 2.23
C. 2.2
D. 2.18

2) A. 1.61
B. 1.57
C. 2
D. 1.19

3) A. 26.3
B. 27
C. 26.8
D. 26.74

4) A. 15
B. 15.65
C. 15.26
D. 15.3

5) A. 23.4
B. 24
C. 23.9
D. 23.99

6) A. 6.54
B. 6.62
C. 6.9
D. 6.5

7) A. 3
B. 2.6
C. 2.18
D. 2.71

8) A. 88
B. 87.81
C. 87.86
D. 87.54

9) A. 23.8
B. 23
C. 23.19
D. 23.97

10) A. 71.57
B. 71.49
C. 71.1
D. 71.79

11) A. 5.8
B. 5.77
C. 5
D. 5.72

12) A. 57.99
B. 57.4
C. 57.3
D. 57.6

13) A. 3.14
B. 3
C. 3.05
D. 3.3

14) A. 36.17
B. 36.52
C. 36.6
D. 36.67

15) A. 4.3
B. 4.6
C. 4
D. 4.2

16) A. 62
B. 61.89
C. 61.86
D. 61.74

17) A. 1.35
B. 2
C. 1.73
D. 1.7

18) A. 27.2
B. 27.38
C. 27.41
D. 27.68

19) A. 6.36
B. 6.7
C. 6.1
D. 6.06

20) A. 1.67
B. 1.15
C. 2
D. 1.7

Ex. B,C,D,A

1. _____

2. _____

3. _____

4. _____

5. _____

6. _____

7. _____

8. _____

9. _____

10. _____

11. _____

12. _____

13. _____

14. _____

15. _____

16. _____

17. _____

18. _____

19. _____

20. _____

Order the numbers from least to greatest

Ex) A. 47.85
B. 47.9
C. 47.33
D. 47.2

1) A. 1.1
B. 1.7
C. 1
D. 1.2

2) A. 7.3
B. 7.65
C. 7.82
D. 8

3) A. 4.6
B. 4.48
C. 5
D. 4.4

4) A. 73.7
B. 73
C. 73.24
D. 73.28

5) A. 1.8
B. 2
C. 1.23
D. 1.3

6) A. 32
B. 31.95
C. 31.6
D. 31.32

7) A. 73.2
B. 73.46
C. 73.6
D. 73

8) A. 50.41
B. 50.7
C. 50.74
D. 50.1

9) A. 7.9
B. 7
C. 7.64
D. 7.86

10) A. 15.55
B. 15.34
C. 15.7
D. 15.8

11) A. 41.53
B. 41.5
C. 41.22
D. 41.82

12) A. 5.3
B. 5.7
C. 5.41
D. 5

13) A. 6.5
B. 6.03
C. 6.84
D. 6.51

14) A. 95.9
B. 95.85
C. 95.1
D. 95.92

15) A. 34.53
B. 34.4
C. 34
D. 34.35

16) A. 4.4
B. 4.36
C. 4.78
D. 4.17

17) A. 1.2
B. 1.1
C. 1.98
D. 2

18) A. 4.18
B. 4.23
C. 4.4
D. 4.95

19) A. 3.53
B. 3.4
C. 3.78
D. 4

20) A. 21.4
B. 21
C. 21.3
D. 21.04

Ex. _D,C,A,B_

1. _____

2. _____

3. _____

4. _____

5. _____

6. _____

7. _____

8. _____

9. _____

10. _____

11. _____

12. _____

13. _____

14. _____

15. _____

16. _____

17. _____

18. _____

19. _____

20. _____

Order the numbers from least to greatest

Ex) A. 8.6
B. 8.41
C. 9
D. 8.88

1) A. 7.22
B. 7.5
C. 7.97
D. 7.8

2) A. 3.57
B. 3.12
C. 4
D. 3.54

3) A. 92.83
B. 93
C. 92.4
D. 92.3

4) A. 24.01
B. 24.27
C. 24.91
D. 24.1

5) A. 5.33
B. 5.91
C. 6
D. 5.64

6) A. 5.6
B. 5.43
C. 5
D. 5.5

7) A. 7.9
B. 7.4
C. 7.44
D. 7.68

8) A. 6
B. 5.88
C. 5.6
D. 5.7

9) A. 69.6
B. 69.06
C. 70
D. 69.28

10) A. 18.93
B. 18
C. 18.32
D. 18.1

11) A. 5.5
B. 5.2
C. 5.81
D. 5

12) A. 13.67
B. 13.39
C. 13.8
D. 13.7

13) A. 76.7
B. 76.6
C. 76.2
D. 77

14) A. 6.1
B. 6.27
C. 6.72
D. 6.6

15) A. 51.55
B. 52
C. 51.72
D. 51.1

16) A. 87.5
B. 87.4
C. 87
D. 87.61

17) A. 9.27
B. 9.5
C. 9.48
D. 9.3

18) A. 64.14
B. 64.1
C. 64.23
D. 64.78

19) A. 20.61
B. 20.4
C. 20.3
D. 20.7

20) A. 3
B. 2.5
C. 2.85
D. 2.2

Ex. _B,A,D,C_

1. _____
2. _____
3. _____
4. _____
5. _____
6. _____
7. _____
8. _____
9. _____
10. _____
11. _____
12. _____
13. _____
14. _____
15. _____
16. _____
17. _____
18. _____
19. _____
20. _____

Answer Key

1

1. 1/2	11. 0
2. 0	12. 1
3. 0	13. 0
4. 1	14. 0
5. 1/2	15. 1
6. 1/2	16. 0
7. 1/2	17. 1
8. 1	18. 0
9. 1/2	19. 1/2
10. 1	20. 1

2

1. 1/2	11. 1/2
2. 1	12. 1
3. 1	13. 0
4. 1	14. 0
5. 1	15. 0
6. 0	16. 1/2
7. 1	17. 1/2
8. 1/2	18. 1
9. 1/2	19. 0
10. 0	20. 1/2

3

1. 0	11. 1
2. 1	12. 0
3. 1/2	13. 1/2
4. 1	14. 1
5. 0	15. 1/2
6. 1	16. 1/2
7. 0	17. 0
8. 1/2	18. 1
9. 0	19. 1
10. 1/2	20. 1/2

4

1. 1/2	11. 1
2. 1	12. 1/2
3. 1	13. 0
4. 0	14. 1/2
5. 1/2	15. 0
6. 0	16. 1
7. 0	17. 1/2
8. 1	18. 0
9. 0	19. 1/2
10. 1	20. 1/2

5

1. 1/2	11. 1
2. 1	12. 1/2
3. 1	13. 1
4. 1	14. 0
5. 0	15. 1/2
6. 1/2	16. 0
7. 0	17. 1
8. 1/2	18. 0
9. 1	19. 0
10. 1/2	20. 1/2

6

1. 1/2	11. 1
2. 0	12. 1
3. 0	13. 0
4. 1/2	14. 1/2
5. 1/2	15. 0
6. 1	16. 0
7. 1	17. 1
8. 1/2	18. 1
9. 1/2	19. 0
10. 1/2	20. 1

7

1. 1/2	11. 0
2. 0	12. 1
3. 0	13. 1
4. 1	14. 1/2
5. 1/2	15. 1
6. 0	16. 1/2
7. 1/2	17. 0
8. 1	18. 1
9. 1	19. 1/2
10. 0	20. 1/2

8

1. 0	11. 1/2
2. 0	12. 0
3. 1/2	13. 1
4. 1	14. 0
5. 1/2	15. 0
6. 1/2	16. 1/2
7. 1	17. 1
8. 1/2	18. 0
9. 1	19. 1/2
10. 1	20. 0

9

1. 0	11. 1/2
2. 1/2	12. 1
3. 0	13. 0
4. 1/2	14. 1/2
5. 0	15. 1
6. 1	16. 0
7. 1	17. 0
8. 1/2	18. 0
9. 1/2	19. 1
10. 1	20. 1/2

10

1. 1/2	11. 0
2. 1	12. 1/2
3. 0	13. 1
4. 1	14. 0
5. 1	15. 1
6. 0	16. 1/2
7. 1/2	17. 1
8. 0	18. 1
9. 1/2	19. 1/2
10. 0	20. 0

11

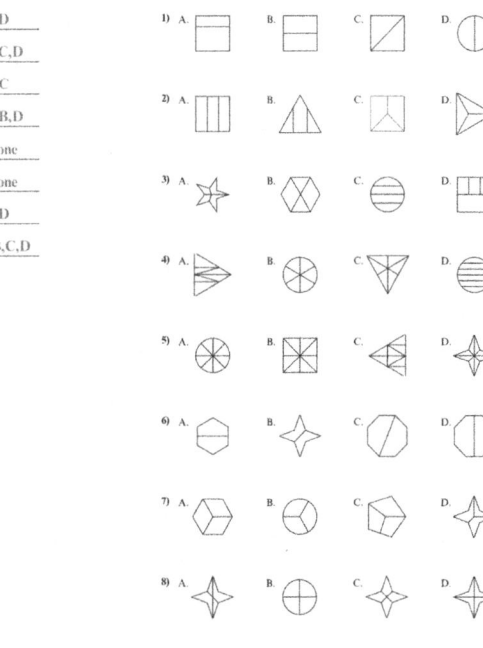

1.	D
2.	B,C,D
3.	C
4.	A,B,D
5.	none
6.	none
7.	D
8.	A,B,C,D

12

1.	B,C,D
2.	A,D
3.	none
4.	B,C
5.	A,B,C,D
6.	A,B,C,D
7.	A,B
8.	B,C,D

13

1) A. B. C. D.
2) A. B. C. D.
3) A. B. C. D.
4) A. B. C. D.
5) A. B. C. D.
6) A. B. C. D.
7) A. B. C. D.
8) A. B. C. D.

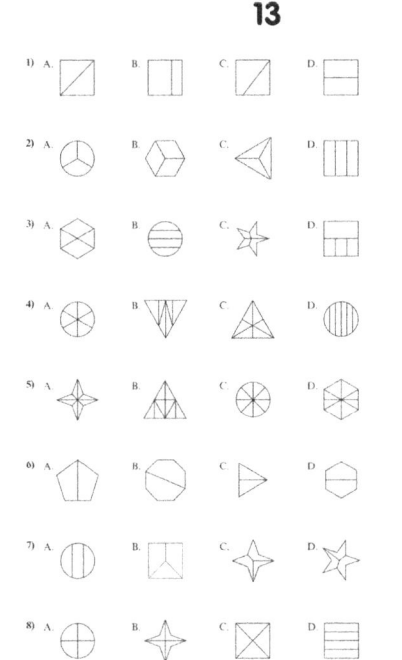

1.   A,D
2.   A,B,C,D
3.   none
4.   A,C
5.   A,B,C
6.   A,B,C,D
7.   none
8.   A,B,C,D

14

1) A. B. C. D.
2) A. B. C. D.
3) A. B. C. D.
4) A. B. C. D.
5) A. B. C. D.
6) A. B. C. D.
7) A. B. C. D.
8) A. B. C. D.

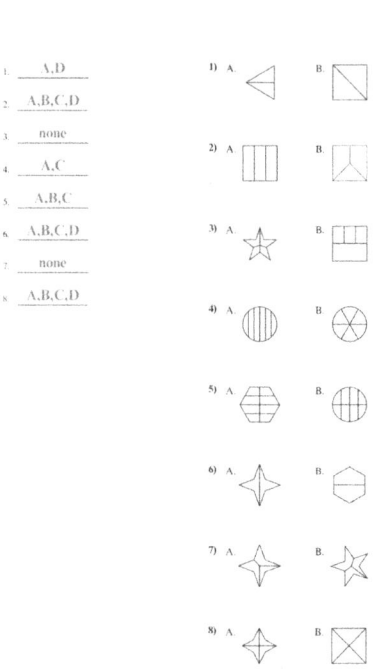
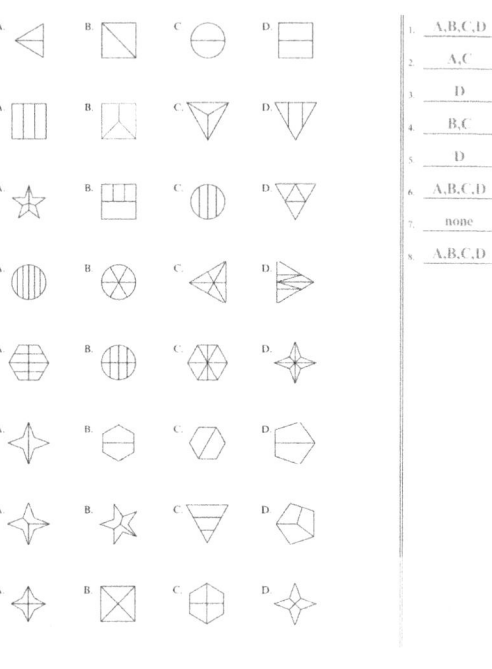

1.   A,B,C,D
2.   A,C
3.   D
4.   B,C
5.   D
6.   A,B,C,D
7.   none
8.   A,B,C,D

15

1) A. B. C. D.
2) A. B. C. D.
3) A. B. C. D.
4) A. B. C. D.
5) A. B. C. D.
6) A. B. C. D.
7) A. B. C. D.
8) A. B. C. D.

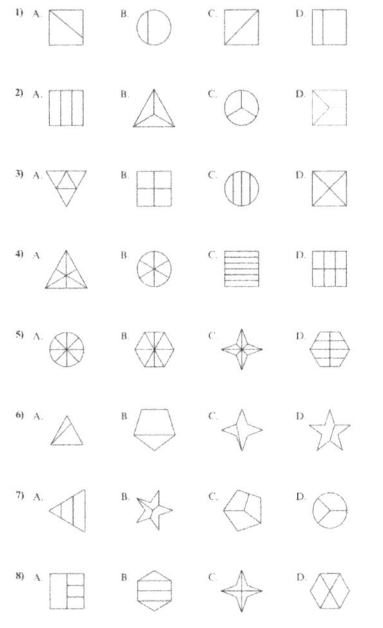

1.   C
2.   A,B,C
3.   A,B,D
4.   A,B,C,D
5.   A,C
6.   none
7.   none
8.   C

16

1) A. B. C. D.
2) A. B. C. D.
3) A. B. C. D.
4) A. B. C. D.
5) A. B. C. D.
6) A. B. C. D.
7) A. B. C. D.
8) A. B. C. D.

1.   A,B,C,D
2.   C
3.   C,D
4.   A,B,C,D
5.   D
6.   B,D
7.   B,C
8.   A,B,C

17

1) A. B. C. D.
2) A. B. C. D.
3) A. B. C. D.
4) A. B. C. D.
5) A. B. C. D.
6) A. B. C. D.
7) A. B. C. D.
8) A. B. C. D.

1. B
2. A,B,C,D
3. A,B,C
4. A,B,C,D
5. A
6. none
7. none
8. A,D

18

1) A. B. C. D.
2) A. B. C. D.
3) A. B. C. D.
4) A. B. C. D.
5) A. B. C. D.
6) A. B. C. D.
7) A. B. C. D.
8) A. B. C. D.

1. A,B,C
2. none
3. A,B,C,D
4. C
5. B,C
6. A,B,C,D
7. A,B,C,D
8. A,B,C,D

19

1) A. B. C. D.
2) A. B. C. D.
3) A. B. C. D.
4) A. B. C. D.
5) A. B. C. D.
6) A. B. C. D.
7) A. B. C. D.
8) A. B. C. D.

1. A,B,C,D
2. none
3. A
4. A,B,D
5. D
6. A,D
7. A,B,C,D
8. A,B,C

20

1) A. B. C. D.
2) A. B. C. D.
3) A. B. C. D.
4) A. B. C. D.
5) A. B. C. D.
6) A. B. C. D.
7) A. B. C. D.
8) A. B. C. D.

1. B
2. A,D
3. none
4. none
5. B,C,D
6. A
7. none
8. A,B,D

21

1. 3/8	11. 5/8
2. 1/8	12. 2/4
3. 4/8	13. 3/6
4. 7/8	14. 4/6
5. 2/8	15. 1/2
6. 5/6	16. 6/8
7. 1/4	17. 2/3
8. 1/3	18. 2/6
9. 3/4	
10. 1/6	

22

1. 3/6	11. 2/6
2. 1/2	12. 2/8
3. 4/6	13. 1/6
4. 2/3	14. 1/8
5. 3/8	15. 5/6
6. 1/3	16. 2/4
7. 4/8	17. 5/8
8. 6/8	18. 3/4
9. 1/4	
10. 7/8	

23

1. 3/4	11. 7/8
2. 3/6	12. 4/6
3. 1/3	13. 5/8
4. 1/4	14. 2/6
5. 1/6	15. 1/8
6. 3/8	16. 2/3
7. 1/2	17. 2/8
8. 6/8	18. 2/4
9. 4/8	
10. 5/6	

24

1. 1/3	11. 2/8
2. 1/4	12. 5/6
3. 3/4	13. 4/8
4. 2/6	14. 7/8
5. 6/8	15. 4/6
6. 3/8	16. 1/8
7. 5/8	17. 2/4
8. 2/3	18. 3/6
9. 1/6	
10. 1/2	

25

1. 7/8
2. 1/8
3. 3/4
4. 4/8
5. 1/2
6. 2/3
7. 6/8
8. 4/6
9. 1/6
10. 5/8
11. 5/6
12. 2/8
13. 1/4
14. 3/8
15. 2/4
16. 3/6
17. 2/6
18. 1/3

26

1. 1/6
2. 2/8
3. 4/8
4. 6/8
5. 7/8
6. 3/4
7. 5/6
8. 2/6
9. 1/8
10. 4/6
11. 1/2
12. 3/6
13. 1/4
14. 2/4
15. 5/8
16. 3/8
17. 2/3
18. 1/3

27

1. 7/8
2. 4/6
3. 2/4
4. 2/3
5. 3/4
6. 2/8
7. 1/3
8. 1/8
9. 1/4
10. 1/6
11. 5/6
12. 1/2
13. 4/8
14. 3/6
15. 6/8
16. 5/8
17. 2/6
18. 3/8

28

1. 2/4
2. 2/8
3. 3/8
4. 3/4
5. 1/3
6. 2/6
7. 1/4
8. 3/6
9. 4/6
10. 1/6
11. 5/8
12. 1/2
13. 2/3
14. 1/8
15. 5/6
16. 7/8
17. 6/8
18. 4/8

29

1. 5/6	11. 1/8
2. 4/6	12. 4/8
3. 1/3	13. 6/8
4. 2/6	14. 3/4
5. 5/8	15. 1/2
6. 2/4	16. 3/8
7. 2/8	17. 1/4
8. 1/6	18. 2/3
9. 7/8	
10. 3/6	

30

1. 1/4	11. 5/8
2. 6/8	12. 3/4
3. 3/6	13. 3/8
4. 1/8	14. 2/3
5. 4/8	15. 7/8
6. 2/6	16. 1/3
7. 1/2	17. 1/6
8. 5/6	18. 2/8
9. 2/4	
10. 4/6	

31

1) 1.41	=	1.41
2) -7.3	>	-7.34
3) 1.87	>	0.187
4) -6.54	>	-6.56
5) 7.48	>	7.42
6) -0.64	<	-0.064
7) -7.09	>	-7.13
8) -9.8	>	-9.85
9) -4.37	>	-4.39
10) 10	>	1
11) 7.8	>	7.79
12) 4.05	>	0.405
13) -7.77	<	-0.777
14) 1.29	>	1.25
15) -5.14	=	-5.14
16) 7.07	>	0.707
17) 0.57	>	0.53
18) 1.45	>	0.145
19) -2.96	<	-0.296
20) -3.36	>	-3.37

32

1) -9.61	<	-0.961
2) -6.5	<	-0.65
3) -5.16	>	-5.18
4) -2.24	=	-2.24
5) 0.86	>	0.086
6) 8.23	>	0.823
7) 1.06	<	1.14
8) 5.35	<	5.42
9) 3.37	>	0.337
10) -0.49	>	-0.51
11) 5.7	>	5.68
12) -3.74	>	-3.75
13) -0.4	<	-0.04
14) 7.19	<	7.23
15) 2.04	<	2.08
16) -9.82	<	-0.982
17) 6.35	>	6.29
18) -9.46	<	-0.946
19) 3.32	<	3.35
20) -8.52	>	-8.59

33

1) 6.23 $<$ 6.26
2) -5.11 $<$ -0.511
3) 8.7 $>$ 0.87
4) 0.39 $>$ 0.039
5) -2.62 $<$ -0.262
6) -4.22 $<$ -4.15
7) 9.9 $=$ 9.9
8) 0.41 $=$ 0.41
9) 2 $>$ 0.2
10) -2.47 $>$ -2.51

11) 5.15 $>$ 5.12
12) 4.88 $>$ 0.488
13) 8.48 $<$ 8.56
14) -6.55 $>$ -6.57
15) -3.22 $=$ -3.22
16) -2.96 $<$ -0.296
17) -9.09 $>$ -9.12
18) -0.46 $<$ -0.38
19) -6.59 $>$ -6.67
20) 2.17 $>$ 0.217

34

1) -5.01 $<$ -4.99
2) -6.89 $<$ -0.689
3) 2.97 $>$ 2.95
4) 7.88 $>$ 0.788
5) 7.38 $>$ 7.35
6) -0.87 $<$ -0.087
7) 3.68 $>$ 0.368
8) 8.35 $=$ 8.35
9) 8.72 $>$ 0.872
10) 3.56 $<$ 3.58

11) 8.57 $>$ 8.55
12) -1.45 $<$ -0.145
13) -3.13 $<$ -0.313
14) -6.81 $>$ -6.82
15) 8.38 $>$ 8.37
16) -8.46 $>$ -8.54
17) -0.68 $<$ -0.67
18) 7.4 $>$ 0.74
19) -5.79 $<$ -5.71
20) -5.73 $<$ -5.71

35

1) -5.31 $<$ -5.3
2) 5.99 $>$ 5.94
3) -0.88 $<$ -0.088
4) 3.77 $>$ 0.377
5) 2.73 $<$ 2.75
6) 6.12 $<$ 6.15
7) 9.51 $>$ 9.48
8) 5.43 $>$ 5.4
9) -2.14 $<$ -0.214
10) 7.87 $>$ 0.787

11) -4.57 $<$ -0.457
12) 9.66 $=$ 9.66
13) -8.68 $<$ -8.66
14) -2.28 $<$ -0.228
15) 1.27 $>$ 0.127
16) -2.25 $>$ -2.31
17) -4.37 $>$ -4.4
18) 5.18 $>$ 5.14
19) -9.92 $<$ -9.9
20) -3.59 $<$ -0.359

36

1) 5.81 $>$ 5.8
2) 6.07 $>$ 6.02
3) -4.62 $<$ -4.54
4) 4.08 $<$ 4.14
5) 2.6 $>$ 0.26
6) -0.42 $<$ -0.38
7) -8.56 $<$ -0.856
8) -2.67 $<$ -2.63
9) 0.71 $>$ 0.071
10) -8.74 $<$ -8.69

11) -6.14 $<$ -0.614
12) 5.21 $>$ 5.13
13) 3.92 $>$ 0.392
14) -8.38 $<$ -0.838
15) 2.24 $<$ 2.28
16) 1.12 $>$ 0.112
17) -4.27 $<$ -0.427
18) -9.66 $>$ -9.7
19) -5.24 $>$ -5.25
20) 3.56 $<$ 3.58

37

1) -7.27 | < | -7.21   11) -5.22 | > | -5.24

2) 7.25 | < | 7.3   12) 5.37 | < | 5.39

3) -4.05 | > | -4.07   13) -5.67 | < | -0.567

4) -9.5 | < | -9.49   14) 2.95 | > | 2.94

5) 2.31 | < | 2.37   15) -2.22 | < | -0.222

6) 4.2 | > | 0.42   16) 6.81 | > | 0.681

7) 0.24 | > | 0.024   17) -8.11 | < | -0.811

8) 2.22 | < | 2.29   18) -0.23 | < | -0.023

9) 4.17 | > | 0.417   19) -6.35 | > | -6.41

10) -3.32 | < | -3.29   20) 3.44 | < | 3.51

38

1) -6.89 | > | -6.9   11) 3.72 | > | 0.372

2) -1.49 | < | -0.149   12) -7.37 | > | -7.4

3) 7.89 | > | 7.85   13) 4.05 | < | 4.09

4) 8.11 | > | 0.811   14) -3.46 | < | -0.346

5) -1.17 | < | -1.16   15) 5.12 | > | 0.512

6) 6.57 | > | 6.56   16) 2.57 | > | 2.51

7) -7.24 | < | -7.2   17) 8.78 | > | 8.71

8) 7.71 | > | 0.771   18) -9.03 | < | -0.903

9) -5.13 | > | -5.19   19) 8.34 | > | 0.834

10) -8.99 | < | -8.96   20) -8.14 | > | -8.17

39

1) 0.95 | < | 1.01   11) -8.59 | < | -0.859

2) 8.85 | > | 8.77   12) 5.11 | > | 5.1

3) -5.49 | < | -0.549   13) -5.94 | < | -5.91

4) -4.45 | < | -0.445   14) 6 | > | 0.6

5) 7.79 | < | 7.84   15) 8.19 | < | 8.24

6) -3.03 | < | -2.95   16) -3.57 | < | -3.56

7) -8.38 | < | -0.838   17) -3.33 | < | -3.26

8) 1.87 | > | 0.187   18) 7.7 | > | 0.77

9) 3.18 | > | 0.318   19) -5.59 | < | -5.54

10) 9.08 | < | 9.13   20) -5.67 | > | -5.68

40

1) 5.53 | < | 5.54   11) -8.94 | > | -8.96

2) -5.78 | > | -5.83   12) 4.66 | > | 4.65

3) 3.5 | > | 0.35   13) -3.85 | < | -3.83

4) 9.65 | = | 9.65   14) -2.48 | > | -2.52

5) -7.41 | < | -7.39   15) 9.03 | < | 9.07

6) -8.97 | < | -8.89   16) -3.04 | > | -3.1

7) -2.24 | < | -2.2   17) -8.25 | < | -0.825

8) 8.2 | > | 0.82   18) 5.4 | > | 0.54

9) -3.03 | < | -0.303   19) 8.4 | > | 0.84

10) 3.58 | > | 0.358   20) 1.33 | > | 0.133

41

96.85 - 43.27 53.58	59.82 - 31.65 28.17	48.69 - 12.39 36.30	69.49 +28.69 98.18	75.83 - 37.85 37.98
51.82 +89.68 141.50	89.89 - 65.33 24.56	97.98 - 92.53 5.45	99.29 +82.34 181.63	30.41 +72.17 102.58
62.14 +98.16 160.30	38.25 +57.81 96.06	72.39 +82.36 154.75	98.32 - 37.92 60.40	57.78 +69.39 127.17
22.39 +54.69 77.08	45.48 - 17.85 27.63	56.34 - 51.58 4.76	48.56 - 40.77 7.79	79.93 +25.38 105.31

42

63.55 - 23.41 40.14	88.98 +87.88 176.86	85.49 +46.31 131.80	94.17 +97.63 191.80	19.38 - 15.57 3.81
37.72 +57.63 95.35	83.37 - 56.74 26.63	68.84 - 52.56 16.28	90.82 - 84.34 6.48	47.37 +27.24 74.61
62.32 - 37.28 25.04	87.87 - 85.33 2.54	70.94 +44.75 115.69	57.22 - 41.42 15.80	10.95 +84.69 95.64
74.14 - 53.23 20.91	62.72 +42.67 105.39	86.42 +87.81 174.23	19.34 +57.83 77.17	43.15 - 14.77 28.38

43

89.29 - 38.61 50.68	89.99 - 70.45 19.54	83.97 +15.35 99.32	94.51 - 33.26 61.25	51.76 +75.97 127.73
85.88 +93.66 179.54	17.78 - 16.41 1.37	29.73 +35.12 64.85	40.16 - 26.24 13.92	52.78 +52.31 105.09
56.11 +63.91 120.02	81.85 +20.83 102.68	47.18 +27.66 74.84	42.75 +87.35 130.10	33.66 - 12.92 20.74
27.11 - 12.63 14.48	46.66 - 15.86 30.80	68.57 - 52.25 16.32	70.61 +28.14 98.75	34.48 - 29.79 4.69

44

49.13 - 17.43 31.70	92.62 - 36.71 55.91	75.48 - 13.94 61.54	86.58 - 14.23 72.35	79.11 +35.41 114.52
97.12 - 80.56 16.56	45.35 - 10.52 34.83	98.94 - 16.97 81.97	60.51 +45.54 106.05	46.35 +81.55 127.90
28.99 +50.33 79.32	90.62 - 81.35 9.27	12.82 +32.78 45.60	34.54 +46.98 81.52	92.99 - 40.97 52.02
62.71 +81.93 144.64	88.92 +50.61 139.53	65.43 - 63.44 1.99	84.33 +53.74 138.07	71.64 +10.25 81.89

45

32.24	19.47	37.55	24.21	66.43
+27.92	+48.53	+79.15	+84.35	- 48.78
60.16	68.00	116.70	108.56	17.65

42.83	11.12	91.98	82.12	54.16
- 38.11	+12.16	- 41.27	- 11.42	+75.56
4.72	23.28	50.71	70.70	129.72

71.54	65.94	60.27	97.36	61.71
+20.66	+24.13	+76.57	- 35.79	- 23.77
92.20	90.07	136.84	61.57	37.94

34.48	57.19	79.25	56.45	80.86
- 10.83	- 34.28	- 42.14	- 15.92	+92.15
23.65	22.91	37.11	40.53	173.01

46

61.46	84.19	18.68	99.87	14.91
- 24.32	- 64.18	+50.36	+68.25	+62.58
37.14	20.01	69.04	168.12	77.49

73.98	45.51	79.31	25.51	35.15
- 20.89	- 25.29	+36.97	+96.36	+72.83
53.09	20.22	116.28	121.87	107.98

73.61	74.77	82.38	86.19	60.24
- 36.48	- 11.38	+93.62	- 67.43	- 52.17
37.13	63.39	176.00	18.76	8.07

63.57	74.11	63.24	48.42	71.32
+96.15	- 70.59	- 44.68	+64.58	+57.77
159.72	3.52	18.56	113.00	129.09

47

53.65	75.69	65.32	75.82	23.82
+71.28	- 72.24	+29.12	- 53.66	- 15.68
124.93	3.45	94.44	22.16	8.14

32.34	31.26	92.45	79.76	66.23
- 24.32	+52.31	- 76.72	+50.65	- 35.51
8.02	83.57	15.73	130.41	30.72

98.64	27.63	81.12	34.43	85.88
- 87.48	+98.63	- 23.19	- 24.73	+77.62
11.16	126.26	57.93	9.70	163.50

19.33	76.68	85.19	87.77	47.65
+75.93	+80.51	- 39.67	+27.92	+96.92
95.26	157.19	45.52	115.69	144.57

48

39.31	52.88	68.59	25.57	61.28
+80.49	+45.36	- 31.67	- 23.38	+68.17
119.80	98.24	36.92	2.19	129.45

68.11	80.81	58.45	90.46	49.29
+26.19	+74.73	+88.63	- 74.64	- 14.57
94.30	155.54	147.08	15.82	34.72

39.59	52.31	65.36	66.17	79.43
- 14.19	- 20.96	+71.24	+99.15	+91.94
25.40	31.35	136.60	165.32	171.37

78.67	43.46	44.67	98.77	88.25
+26.83	- 21.68	- 43.86	- 62.22	- 22.12
105.50	21.78	0.81	36.55	66.13

49

58.96 − 18.24 = 40.72	25.47 + 46.16 = 71.63	82.41 − 69.42 = 12.99	65.81 − 47.88 = 17.93	20.84 + 20.23 = 41.07
16.58 − 11.69 = 4.89	12.45 + 90.75 = 103.20	58.42 − 49.49 = 8.93	41.41 + 46.74 = 88.15	94.12 + 92.92 = 187.04
52.83 + 80.94 = 133.77	89.79 − 73.56 = 16.23	44.78 − 26.69 = 18.09	91.62 − 73.27 = 18.35	11.63 + 46.26 = 57.89
65.73 + 66.57 = 132.30	80.12 − 52.22 = 27.90	74.69 − 10.11 = 64.58	60.42 + 36.38 = 96.80	57.51 + 23.15 = 80.66

50

85.83 + 15.92 = 101.75	32.57 + 72.96 = 105.53	85.91 + 55.29 = 141.20	63.51 − 44.57 = 18.94	60.88 − 24.79 = 36.09
80.41 + 79.58 = 159.99	24.78 − 16.31 = 8.47	69.58 − 54.92 = 14.66	32.93 − 24.64 = 8.29	98.55 − 28.48 = 70.07
81.25 + 29.36 = 110.61	30.32 − 21.22 = 9.10	22.89 + 72.97 = 95.86	97.62 − 72.44 = 25.18	82.96 + 95.69 = 178.65
56.65 − 21.93 = 34.72	38.91 + 76.55 = 115.46	32.85 + 30.81 = 63.66	86.45 − 57.85 = 28.60	91.36 + 18.14 = 109.50

51

Ex) A. 34 B. 33.85 C. 33.22 D. 33.8
1) A. 73.96 B. 73.5 C. 73.4 D. 73.1
2) A. 3.29 B. 3.55 C. 3.6 D. 3.86
3) A. 4.19 B. 4.27 C. 4.6 D. 5
4) A. 5.7 B. 5.2 C. 5.6 D. 5.25
5) A. 22.4 B. 22.8 C. 22.3 D. 22.91
6) A. 11.59 B. 11.46 C. 12 D. 11.6
7) A. 8 B. 7.96 C. 7.35 D. 7.63
8) A. 3 B. 2.57 C. 2.9 D. 2.2
9) A. 9.17 B. 9.5 C. 9.9 D. 10
10) A. 75.6 B. 75.9 C. 75.8 D. 75.22
11) A. 83.11 B. 83.6 C. 83.16 D. 83.4
12) A. 3.8 B. 4 C. 3.86 D. 3.9
13) A. 72.5 B. 72.59 C. 72.4 D. 72.3
14) A. 44.9 B. 44.5 C. 44.53 D. 44
15) A. 4.2 B. 5 C. 4.99 D. 4.22
16) A. 7.3 B. 7.01 C. 8 D. 7.8
17) A. 3.68 B. 3.5 C. 3.7 D. 3.88
18) A. 14.62 B. 14.5 C. 14.87 D. 14.76
19) A. 65.8 B. 66 C. 65.2 D. 65.7
20) A. 2.25 B. 2.52 C. 2.2 D. 2.1

Ex. C,D,B,A
1. D,C,B,A
2. A,B,C,D
3. A,B,C,D
4. B,D,C,A
5. C,A,B,D
6. B,A,D,C
7. C,D,B,A
8. D,B,C,A
9. A,B,C,D
10. D,A,C,B
11. A,C,D,B
12. A,C,D,B
13. D,C,A,B
14. D,B,C,A
15. A,D,C,B
16. B,A,D,C
17. B,A,C,D
18. B,A,D,C
19. C,D,A,B
20. D,C,A,B

52

Ex) A. 93.56 B. 94 C. 93.73 D. 93.2
1) A. 64.2 B. 64.8 C. 64.15 D. 64.84
2) A. 53.4 B. 53.22 C. 53.67 D. 53.42
3) A. 4.7 B. 5 C. 4.9 D. 4.56
4) A. 9.2 B. 9.18 C. 9 D. 9.7
5) A. 6.6 B. 6.29 C. 6.4 D. 6.17
6) A. 5.1 B. 5.4 C. 5.9 D. 5.5
7) A. 10.41 B. 10.4 C. 10.46 D. 10
8) A. 8.9 B. 8.48 C. 8.4 D. 8.7
9) A. 84.67 B. 84.42 C. 84.4 D. 84
10) A. 87.8 B. 88 C. 87.62 D. 87.6
11) A. 90 B. 89.9 C. 89.49 D. 89.5
12) A. 3.42 B. 3 C. 3.8 D. 3.94
13) A. 3.94 B. 3.48 C. 3.8 D. 3.84
14) A. 1 B. 1.27 C. 1.3 D. 1.2
15) A. 8.75 B. 8.48 C. 8.6 D. 8.9
16) A. 49.9 B. 49.22 C. 49.2 D. 49.61
17) A. 96.34 B. 96 C. 96.4 D. 96.9
18) A. 73 B. 72.59 C. 72.99 D. 72.86
19) A. 9.78 B. 9.43 C. 10 D. 9.7
20) A. 3 B. 2.2 C. 2.5 D. 2.42

Ex. D,A,C,B
1. C,A,B,D
2. B,A,D,C
3. D,A,C,B
4. C,B,A,D
5. D,B,C,A
6. A,B,D,C
7. D,B,A,C
8. C,B,D,A
9. D,C,B,A
10. D,C,A,B
11. C,D,B,A
12. B,A,C,D
13. B,C,D,A
14. A,D,B,C
15. B,C,A,D
16. C,B,D,A
17. B,A,C,D
18. B,D,C,A
19. B,D,A,C
20. B,D,C,A

53

Ex) A. 4.77 B. 4.62 C. 5 D. 4.1
1) A. 76.57 B. 77 C. 76.6 D. 76.66
2) A. 9.59 B. 9.2 C. 9.58 D. 9.92
3) A. 39.9 B. 39.17 C. 39.26 D. 39.56
4) A. 28.4 B. 28.1 C. 29 D. 28.24
5) A. 5.58 B. 5.5 C. 5.62 D. 5.7
6) A. 54.4 B. 54.52 C. 54.45 D. 54.7
7) A. 54.68 B. 54.3 C. 54.04 D. 54.5
8) A. 8.84 B. 8.59 C. 8.1 D. 8.4
9) A. 7.18 B. 7.7 C. 7.79 D. 7.1
10) A. 59.75 B. 59.3 C. 59.6 D. 59.49
11) A. 96.78 B. 96.55 C. 96.8 D. 96.6
12) A. 6.12 B. 6.2 C. 6.8 D. 6.17
13) A. 5.2 B. 5.15 C. 5.45 D. 5.52
14) A. 75 B. 74.45 C. 74.44 D. 74.59
15) A. 85.5 B. 85.4 C. 85.01 D. 85.79
16) A. 6.48 B. 6.67 C. 6.7 D. 6.27
17) A. 6.32 B. 6.3 C. 6.18 D. 6
18) A. 9.3 B. 9.66 C. 9.58 D. 10
19) A. 2.31 B. 2.4 C. 2.32 D. 2.1
20) A. 3.7 B. 3.72 C. 3.6 D. 3.2

Ex. D,B,A,C
1. A,C,D,B
2. B,C,A,D
3. B,C,D,A
4. B,D,A,C
5. B,A,C,D
6. A,C,B,D
7. C,B,D,A
8. C,D,B,A
9. D,A,B,C
10. B,D,C,A
11. B,D,A,C
12. A,D,B,C
13. B,A,C,D
14. C,B,D,A
15. C,B,A,D
16. D,A,B,C
17. D,C,B,A
18. A,C,B,D
19. D,A,C,B
20. D,C,A,B

54

Ex) A. 51.9 B. 52 C. 51.13 D. 51.7
1) A. 6.73 B. 7 C. 6.45 D. 6.5
2) A. 59.6 B. 59.03 C. 59.7 D. 59.17
3) A. 21.4 B. 21.49 C. 21 D. 21.89
4) A. 91.72 B. 91.9 C. 92 D. 91.58
5) A. 7.8 B. 7 C. 7.88 D. 7.44
6) A. 23.18 B. 23.53 C. 23.48 D. 23.9
7) A. 42.64 B. 42.6 C. 42.3 D. 42.42
8) A. 5.74 B. 6 C. 5.88 D. 5.82
9) A. 30 B. 30.13 C. 30.4 D. 30.3
10) A. 48.3 B. 48.94 C. 48.4 D. 48
11) A. 2.7 B. 2.8 C. 2.3 D. 2.82
12) A. 47.5 B. 47.7 C. 48 D. 47.53
13) A. 37.05 B. 37.9 C. 37.72 D. 37.4
14) A. 2.5 B. 2.2 C. 2.93 D. 2.83
15) A. 64 B. 63.36 C. 63.3 D. 63.4
16) A. 11.05 B. 11.56 C. 12 D. 11.54
17) A. 90.95 B. 91 C. 90.54 D. 90.1
18) A. 7.7 B. 8 C. 7.41 D. 7.92
19) A. 9.48 B. 9.56 C. 9.4 D. 9.2
20) A. 63.95 B. 63.3 C. 63.7 D. 63.1

Ex. C,D,A,B
1. C,D,A,B
2. B,D,A,C
3. C,A,B,D
4. D,A,B,C
5. B,D,A,C
6. A,C,B,D
7. C,D,B,A
8. A,D,C,B
9. A,B,D,C
10. D,A,C,B
11. C,A,B,D
12. A,D,B,C
13. A,D,C,B
14. B,A,D,C
15. C,B,D,A
16. A,D,B,C
17. D,C,A,B
18. C,A,D,B
19. D,C,A,B
20. D,B,C,A

55

Ex) A. 68.1 B. 68.47 C. 68.4 D. 68.43
1) A. 7 B. 7.4 C. 7.35 D. 7.5
2) A. 89.95 B. 89.8 C. 89.4 D. 89.37
3) A. 1.87 B. 1.9 C. 1.3 D. 2
4) A. 96.8 B. 96.81 C. 96.5 D. 97
5) A. 4.17 B. 4.93 C. 4.8 D. 4.7
6) A. 2.18 B. 2.02 C. 2.7 D. 2.38
7) A. 66.26 B. 66.5 C. 66.61 D. 67
8) A. 37.3 B. 37.58 C. 38 D. 37.22
9) A. 62 B. 61.9 C. 61.85 D. 61.6
10) A. 38.89 B. 38 C. 38.8 D. 38.08
11) A. 46 B. 46.59 C. 46.93 D. 46.89
12) A. 90.1 B. 90.2 C. 90.4 D. 90.63
13) A. 2 B. 2.83 C. 2.2 D. 2.3
14) A. 24.9 B. 24 C. 24.33 D. 24.5
15) A. 97.21 B. 97.42 C. 97.4 D. 97
16) A. 26 B. 25.74 C. 25.9 D. 25.1
17) A. 74.3 B. 74.7 C. 74.9 D. 74.73
18) A. 3.9 B. 3 C. 3.3 D. 3.1
19) A. 8.9 B. 8 C. 8.54 D. 8.51
20) A. 4.12 B. 4.3 C. 4.93 D. 4.1

Ex. A,C,D,B
1. A,C,B,D
2. D,C,B,A
3. C,A,B,D
4. C,A,B,D
5. A,D,C,B
6. B,A,D,C
7. A,B,C,D
8. D,A,B,C
9. D,C,B,A
10. B,D,C,A
11. A,B,D,C
12. A,B,C,D
13. A,C,D,B
14. B,C,D,A
15. D,A,C,B
16. D,B,C,A
17. A,B,D,C
18. B,D,C,A
19. B,D,C,A
20. D,A,B,C

56

Ex) A. 39.53 B. 39.3 C. 39.22 D. 39.9
1) A. 3.9 B. 3.95 C. 3.7 D. 3.74
2) A. 20.19 B. 20 C. 20.4 D. 20.6
3) A. 3.4 B. 3 C. 3.24 D. 3.9
4) A. 36.8 B. 36.1 C. 36.23 D. 37
5) A. 1.3 B. 1.37 C. 1.5 D. 1.2
6) A. 27.42 B. 27.88 C. 27.7 D. 27
7) A. 2.55 B. 2.6 C. 2.3 D. 2.67
8) A. 55.6 B. 55.56 C. 55.8 D. 55.2
9) A. 6.59 B. 7 C. 6.6 D. 6.5
10) A. 26.1 B. 26.86 C. 26.51 D. 26.3
11) A. 46.6 B. 46.19 C. 46.8 D. 47
12) A. 7.4 B. 7.3 C. 7.5 D. 7.19
13) A. 8.23 B. 8.7 C. 8 D. 8.4
14) A. 9 B. 8.99 C. 8.61 D. 8.64
15) A. 7.9 B. 7.2 C. 7.04 D. 7.73
16) A. 28.8 B. 28.6 C. 28.5 D. 28.9
17) A. 30.2 B. 30.37 C. 30.82 D. 30.71
18) A. 60.3 B. 61 C. 60.5 D. 60.71
19) A. 61.9 B. 61.59 C. 61.84 D. 61.91
20) A. 7.6 B. 7.47 C. 7 D. 7.8

Ex. C,B,A,D
1. C,D,A,B
2. B,A,C,D
3. B,C,A,D
4. B,C,A,D
5. D,A,B,C
6. D,A,C,B
7. C,A,B,D
8. D,B,A,C
9. D,A,C,B
10. A,D,C,B
11. B,A,C,D
12. D,B,A,C
13. C,A,D,B
14. C,D,B,A
15. C,B,D,A
16. C,B,A,D
17. A,B,D,C
18. A,C,D,B
19. B,C,A,D
20. C,B,A,D

57

Ex) A. 5.17 B. 5.95 C. 6 D. 5.9	**1)** A. 23.3 B. 23.4 C. 23.9 D. 23.26	**2)** A. 7.5 B. 7.65 C. 7.97 D. 7.14	Ex. A,D,B,C
			1. D,A,B,C
			2. D,A,B,C
3) A. 18.41 B. 18.83 C. 19 D. 18.5	**4)** A. 14.36 B. 14.4 C. 14.86 D. 14.7	**5)** A. 62.24 B. 62.49 C. 62.4 D. 62.7	3. A,D,B,C
			4. A,B,D,C
			5. A,C,B,D
6) A. 1.72 B. 1.74 C. 1.52 D. 1.36	**7)** A. 2.5 B. 2.4 C. 2.12 D. 2.7	**8)** A. 73.75 B. 73.2 C. 74 D. 73.17	6. D,C,A,B
			7. C,B,A,D
			8. D,B,A,C
9) A. 3.42 B. 3.7 C. 3.2 D. 4	**10)** A. 19.18 B. 19.2 C. 19.42 D. 19	**11)** A. 29 B. 28.26 C. 28.5 D. 28.7	9. C,A,B,D
			10. D,A,B,C
			11. B,C,D,A
12) A. 97.6 B. 97.52 C. 97.95 D. 97.7	**13)** A. 9 B. 8.3 C. 8.7 D. 8.99	**14)** A. 50 B. 49.4 C. 49.83 D. 49.5	12. B,A,D,C
			13. B,C,D,A
			14. B,D,C,A
15) A. 29.92 B. 30 C. 29.7 D. 29.5	**16)** A. 9.5 B. 9.6 C. 9.57 D. 9.1	**17)** A. 3.6 B. 3.3 C. 3.39 D. 3.8	15. D,C,A,B
			16. D,A,C,B
			17. B,C,A,D
18) A. 4.4 B. 4.12 C. 4.41 D. 4.5	**19)** A. 24.92 B. 24.4 C. 24.28 D. 24.3	**20)** A. 7.21 B. 7.5 C. 7.4 D. 7	18. B,A,C,D
			19. C,D,B,A
			20. D,A,C,B

58

Ex) A. 68 B. 67.3 C. 67.6 D. 67.89	**1)** A. 2.1 B. 2.23 C. 2.2 D. 2.18	**2)** A. 1.61 B. 1.57 C. 2 D. 1.19	Ex. B,C,D,A
			1. A,D,C,B
			2. D,B,A,C
3) A. 26.3 B. 27 C. 26.8 D. 26.74	**4)** A. 15 B. 15.65 C. 15.26 D. 15.3	**5)** A. 23.4 B. 24 C. 23.9 D. 23.99	3. A,D,C,B
			4. A,C,D,B
			5. A,C,D,B
6) A. 6.54 B. 6.62 C. 6.9 D. 6.5	**7)** A. 3 B. 2.6 C. 2.18 D. 2.71	**8)** A. 88 B. 87.81 C. 87.86 D. 87.54	6. D,A,B,C
			7. C,B,D,A
			8. D,B,C,A
9) A. 23.8 B. 23 C. 23.19 D. 23.97	**10)** A. 71.57 B. 71.49 C. 71.1 D. 71.79	**11)** A. 5.8 B. 5.77 C. 5 D. 5.72	9. B,C,A,D
			10. C,B,A,D
			11. C,D,B,A
12) A. 57.99 B. 57.4 C. 57.3 D. 57.6	**13)** A. 3.14 B. 3 C. 3.05 D. 3.3	**14)** A. 36.17 B. 36.52 C. 36.6 D. 36.67	12. C,B,D,A
			13. B,C,A,D
			14. A,B,C,D
15) A. 4.3 B. 4.6 C. 4 D. 4.2	**16)** A. 62 B. 61.89 C. 61.86 D. 61.74	**17)** A. 1.35 B. 2 C. 1.73 D. 1.7	15. C,D,A,B
			16. D,C,B,A
			17. A,D,C,B
18) A. 27.2 B. 27.38 C. 27.41 D. 27.68	**19)** A. 6.36 B. 6.7 C. 6.1 D. 6.06	**20)** A. 1.67 B. 1.15 C. 2 D. 1.7	18. A,B,C,D
			19. D,C,A,B
			20. B,A,D,C

59

Ex) A. 47.85 B. 47.9 C. 47.33 D. 47.2	**1)** A. 1.1 B. 1.7 C. 1 D. 1.2	**2)** A. 7.3 B. 7.65 C. 7.82 D. 8	Ex. D,C,A,B
			1. C,A,D,B
			2. A,B,C,D
3) A. 4.6 B. 4.48 C. 5 D. 4.4	**4)** A. 73.7 B. 73 C. 73.24 D. 73.28	**5)** A. 1.8 B. 2 C. 1.23 D. 1.3	3. D,B,A,C
			4. B,C,D,A
			5. C,D,A,B
6) A. 32 B. 31.95 C. 31.6 D. 31.32	**7)** A. 73.2 B. 73.46 C. 73.6 D. 73	**8)** A. 50.41 B. 50.7 C. 50.74 D. 50.1	6. D,C,B,A
			7. D,A,B,C
			8. D,A,B,C
9) A. 7.9 B. 7 C. 7.64 D. 7.86	**10)** A. 15.55 B. 15.34 C. 15.7 D. 15.8	**11)** A. 41.53 B. 41.5 C. 41.22 D. 41.82	9. B,C,D,A
			10. B,A,C,D
			11. C,B,A,D
12) A. 5.3 B. 5.7 C. 5.41 D. 5	**13)** A. 6.5 B. 6.03 C. 6.84 D. 6.51	**14)** A. 95.9 B. 95.85 C. 95.1 D. 95.92	12. D,A,C,B
			13. B,A,D,C
			14. C,B,A,D
15) A. 34.53 B. 34.4 C. 34 D. 34.35	**16)** A. 4.4 B. 4.36 C. 4.78 D. 4.17	**17)** A. 1.2 B. 1.1 C. 1.98 D. 2	15. C,D,B,A
			16. D,B,A,C
			17. B,A,C,D
18) A. 4.18 B. 4.23 C. 4.4 D. 4.95	**19)** A. 3.53 B. 3.4 C. 3.78 D. 4	**20)** A. 21.4 B. 21 C. 21.3 D. 21.04	18. A,B,C,D
			19. B,A,C,D
			20. B,D,C,A

60

Ex) A. 8.6 B. 8.41 C. 9 D. 8.88	**1)** A. 7.22 B. 7.5 C. 7.97 D. 7.8	**2)** A. 3.57 B. 3.12 C. 4 D. 3.54	Ex. B,A,D,C
			1. A,B,D,C
			2. B,D,A,C
3) A. 92.83 B. 93 C. 92.4 D. 92.3	**4)** A. 24.01 B. 24.27 C. 24.91 D. 24.1	**5)** A. 5.33 B. 5.91 C. 6 D. 5.64	3. D,C,A,B
			4. A,D,B,C
			5. A,D,B,C
6) A. 5.6 B. 5.43 C. 5 D. 5.5	**7)** A. 7.9 B. 7.4 C. 7.44 D. 7.68	**8)** A. 6 B. 5.88 C. 5.6 D. 5.7	6. C,B,D,A
			7. B,C,D,A
			8. C,D,B,A
9) A. 69.6 B. 69.06 C. 70 D. 69.28	**10)** A. 18.93 B. 18 C. 18.32 D. 18.1	**11)** A. 5.5 B. 5.2 C. 5.81 D. 5	9. B,D,A,C
			10. B,D,C,A
			11. D,B,A,C
12) A. 13.67 B. 13.39 C. 13.8 D. 13.7	**13)** A. 76.7 B. 76.6 C. 76.2 D. 77	**14)** A. 6.1 B. 6.27 C. 6.72 D. 6.6	12. B,A,D,C
			13. C,B,A,D
			14. A,B,D,C
15) A. 51.55 B. 52 C. 51.72 D. 51.1	**16)** A. 87.5 B. 87.4 C. 87 D. 87.61	**17)** A. 9.27 B. 9.5 C. 9.48 D. 9.3	15. D,A,C,B
			16. C,B,A,D
			17. A,D,C,B
18) A. 64.14 B. 64.1 C. 64.23 D. 64.78	**19)** A. 20.61 B. 20.4 C. 20.3 D. 20.7	**20)** A. 3 B. 2.5 C. 2.85 D. 2.2	18. B,A,C,D
			19. C,B,A,D
			20. D,B,C,A

Made in the USA
Monee, IL
07 July 2026

56545680R00046